Best Wishes,
Ann Pate
2-17-11

FORT CHADBOURNE

A Military Post
A Family Heritage

Ann Pate

H.V. Chapman & Sons
Since 1947

1st Edition

Pate, Ann
Fort Chadbourne
A Military Post
A Family Heritage
          ISBN 978-0-9830180-1-8

Photographs property of Lana Richards
and the Fort Chadbourne Foundation

John Y. Rankin photograph courtesy of Ruth Lyle

Schuchard Lithograph with permission of the
Texas State Library & Archives Commission

Acknowledgements

To Lana and Garland Richards
Two of the best friends I have ever had.
Thank you for allowing me to be a part
of your dream. It has been a privilege to serve
as one of your Board of Directors,
and work along side you each day in
restoring and presenting Fort Chadbourne
to all who enter its doors.

To Mary "Sug" Lawhon
A very special lady who I truly admire.
Thank you for your help.

To James Kenney
Many thanks for both your help and words
of encouragement along the way.

To Randall
My husband who kept urging me on,
and telling me over and over,
"You can do this!"
Thank you for always having faith in me.

To my fellow Fort Chadbourne Board of Directors
It's been a pleasure to serve with you, and watch
Fort Chadbourne emerge as a new Star in Texas.

Foreword

The Fort Chadbourne project is something that should not have happened. Lana and I were told from the beginning that we could not accomplish the goals set by the Board of Directors, at the first meeting in 1999. We were told that the only way to restore a historic site was to relinquish control of the fort to a federal or state agency, "who had funding and expertise to do a project like this."

Six of ten stone buildings have been restored. All of the ruins have been stabilized. Six of the buildings have had archeological excavations and reports published on them.

Every donation to Fort Chadbourne goes toward a project to better this historic site. There has been more historic preservation take place at Fort Chadbourne, per dollar spent, than any where in the State of Texas.

Half the work that has been done at the Fort has been in the office. Grant writing, fundraising, event planning, and research. There is no job description.

We do what is needed to be done that day to be able to survive until the next day.

Ann Pate has been an integral part of the Fort since 2005, and has become the leading authority on Fort Chadbourne History. No one is better qualified to present the history of this Fort than Ann.

Two years ago I asked Ann to write the History of Fort Chadbourne. At that time she was organizing the historical data compiled from the National Archives, along with local histories, fort files and any information found concerning Fort Chadbourne. She was the lady for the job. She had participated in the archeological investigations on the buildings, and had seen the restoration program at Fort Chadbourne completed.

About a year ago, Ann walked up to my desk without saying a word, and laid the outline for this book in front of me. She was hooked! After a year of strange sounds, a lot of mumbling, and a few outbursts, this book was ready to take to the publishers.

Ann has taken the bits and pieces of the Fort Chadbourne puzzle, and carefully placed each part in place. She filled the missing spaces with stories, archeology, muster rolls, medical reports, photographs, diaries, and B.S. She has painted the most complete picture of Fort Chadbourne ever presented.

Enjoy the book. It is a work of art!

Garland Richards
President
Fort Chadbourne Foundation

Preface

When Garland Richards first began to urge me to write this book about Fort Chadbourne, I quickly learned that this historic old post is as rich in family history as it is in military history. So, it is impossible to tell one story without telling the other. They intertwine, and are actually one and the same.

I have often asked myself this question, "Would the historic military post Fort Chadbourne still be around today if Thomas and Lucinda Odom had not been the ones to purchase it, establish a ranch headquarters, and then turn it into a family legacy passed down through generation's of Odom's, Wylie's and Richards'?" Probably not.

Fort Chadbourne, the military post, served only some fifteen years, but Chadbourne Ranch has endured for over 125 years because a family built it on strength, endurance, and hard work. Many view this family as an oil rich lineage that simply had it handed to them. Their ancestry says differently. Thomas Odom, and his descendants, worked hard for what they built, and then by chance got lucky in 1949 when

vii

the first oil well the "Sallie Odom" was drilled. If you truly know the family, you realize that Chadbourne Oil is not who they are, it is only a part of what makes up this historic family.

Even after oil was discovered, the family continued to ranch, use their money wisely, and generously benefit many charitable organizations, including the Fort Chadbourne Foundation. If not for Garland Richards, the great great great grandson of Thomas Odom, and his wife Lana, the restoration of this 1852 garrison may never have reached the potential we see today.

There is no doubt that Thomas Odom would be very proud to know his vision of Fort Chadbourne in owning land, and great prosperity, still stands today. Although early generations before Richards viewed Fort Chadbourne strictly as a working ranch, choosing to overlook its historical value, time has a way of changing our point of view.

That is the way of Fort Chadbourne. A military post becomes a ranch. Through the years it grows and thrives, making itself part of history. Later Chadbourne Ranch too becomes of historical significance, and then gradually it returns to the roots from which it was formed, known as Fort Chadbourne.

So, I could not simply write about a single military post located in West Texas. I felt the need to convey the impact of the military footsteps left here, the ranching heritage as it rode through, and last but not least, how Thomas Odom and his descendants have added to the archives of our Texas History.

Welcome to "Fort Chadbourne".

Ann Pate

Table of Contents

The Military Years   **Page**

Chapter I   Find a Location 3

Chapter II   Establish Fort Chadbourne..........................17

Chapter III   Dealing with Indians...................................29

Chapter IV   A. B. Gray 45

Chapter V   Military Burial 53

Chapter VI   J.K.F. Mansfield and A.G. Miller Reports..........61

Chapter VII   1st Lt. T.A. Washington Takes Inventory..........73

Chapter VIII   1st Lt. E.D. Phillips Building Descriptions.........85

Chapter IX   Surrender of Fort Chadbourne....................105

Chapter X   Sidney Green Davidson.............................115

Chapter XI   Dove Creek...127

Chapter XII   Re-Establish Fort Chadbourne....................133

Chapter XIII   Horse Race...147

Chapter XIV   Trade...153

Chapter XV   Assistant Surgeon Ebenezer Swift...............161

Chapter XVI   Thirteen Arrows..167

Chapter XVII   Other Medical Personnel...........................177

Chapter XVIII   Butterfield Stage Station...........................189

Chapter XIX   Samuel Maverick.......................................205

The Family Heritage   **Page**

Chapter XX   Thomas Lawson Odom.............................217

Chapter XXI   Ranching..229

Chapter XXII   Conda Wylie...241

The Restoration

Chapter XXIII   Form a Foundation, Reconstruct a Fort 249

                      Board of Directors....................................279

Chapter XXIV   Hot Off the Press................................... 281

General Information

Fort Chadbourne Roster of Federal Troops.............................293

Fort Chadbourne Roster of Texas Regimental Troops............303

Fort Chadbourne Mean Strength.......................................305

Fort Chadbourne Commanders... 307

Fort Chadbourne Medal of Honor Recipients.......................309

Fort Chadbourne Deceased...311

Bibliography...315

Endnotes...321

Index...327

Illustrations

The Military Years   **Page**

Texas Frontier Forts Map..15

Layout of Building's by Miller...71

Layout of Building's by Mansfield....................................72

Description of Buildings by Phillips.................................. 94

Butterfield Stage Stop Schedule.....................................203

Schuchard Lithograph..204

The Family Heritage

Benjamin Warren..228

Thomas Lawson Odom..235

Garland and Sallie Odom..236

Conda Holt Wylie...237

Conda and Nell Richards...238

Garland and Lana Richards..239

Restoration

Roberta Cole Johnson..258

Charles and Joy Blake..259

Barracks Before..265

Barracks During..266

Barracks After...267

Fountain House Before.......................................268

Fountain House After..269

Double Officer's Quarters Before.....................270

Double Officer's Quarters After.......................271

Butterfield Stage Stop Before..........................272

Butterfield Stage Stop After.............................273

Root Cellar Before and After............................274

Visitor's Center..275

Artifacts..276

Artifacts..277

Signage...278

Fort Chadbourne
The Military Years

On May 9, 1846, 2nd Lt. Theodore Lincoln Chadbourne[1], a West Point cadet, lost his life in the Mexican War at the Battle of Resaca de la Palma. He would never know his name would forever live on and become infamous with a Texas military post named in his honor. On October 25, 1852, by Special Order 46, Headquarters, 8th Department, this post would officially be declared Fort Chadbourne.

Chapter 1

Find a Location

Following the Mexican War the country was in a relatively peaceful state. The eastern states were somewhat "civilized", but the Wild West was still awaiting her turn. In 1849, when word got back that gold had been discovered in California there was a massive push of Easterners to cross much of this unchartered territory to find their fortunes. The allure of owning land, and striking it rich, sent a progression of both young and old, across this harsh and unforgiving land. They loaded as many of their worldly possessions as would fit into a small and crowded covered wagon, along with hopes and dreams of a better life out west. While facing the scare of Indian attack, rain storms, sand storms, scorching heat, freezing cold, lack of water, food, and disease they forged ahead.

This led the federal government into a plan of action from 1849 to 1852, to place a series of forts in West Texas. These garrisons would lend stabilization to the frontier, and form a line of protection from the hostile Indian raids on these brave pioneers. The idea was to show a strong military presence, which in turn would intimidate the Native American's. Assuming they would quickly bow to governmental authority in order to protect the rights of its citizens, the Federal Government pictured friendly relations hastily being established between military and Indian. It would not proceed so smoothly.

During this time, Indian Agent Robert Simpson Neighbors[2] sponsored a law in the Fourth Texas Legislature, for establishing Indian Reservations. He would work diligently over the next several years to provide a safeguard for the Comanche's and Kiowa's, while still defending the rights of the settlers.

Other than Fort Martin Scott established 1848 near Fredericksburg, Texas, the first United States Army Forts established in 1849 were in East Texas. They included Forts Worth, Graham, Gates, and Croghan. These forts ran from present day Fort Worth, Texas, following a line southwest to Burnett, Texas. The next line of forts in 1851 pushed the line farther west and included Forts Belknap, located in northeast Texas, Phantom Hill near Abilene, Texas, and Mason located in the hill country of Texas. Fort McKavett, near present day Menard, Texas would follow in 1852, along with Forts Chadbourne, located north of Bronte, Terrett near Sonora, and Clark located at Del Rio, Texas. (See Fig. 1)

Brevet[3] Major General Persifor F. Smith[4], Commander of the 8th Military Department in San Antonio at the time, had the authority to select new sites for these posts. There were three considerations: 1) the protection of the inhabitants of Texas, 2) the defense of Mexican territory against Indians in the United States, and 3) economy and facility in supporting the troops, particularly in regard to forage and fuel.[5]

One such earlier site, Camp Johnston, named for Brigadier General Joseph Eggleston Johnston[6], was the precursor to Fort Chadbourne. It was located between the Middle and North Concho, near present day San Angelo, in Tom Green County.

Department Commander Bvt. Major General Persifor Smith issued Order No. 95, on December 16, 1851, directing the 8th U. S. Infantry to move from points east to west. The eastern military posts would be abandoned, while establishing the new western posts, including Fort Chadbourne. The right wing would be located near the Concho River at Camp Johnston, the left wing toward the San Saba River.[7]

On April 18, 1852, command of Camp Johnston and the right wing of the 8th U. S. Infantry were assumed by Colonel John Garland. From the beginning, as he did most things, Garland intensely questioned the location of the future site of Fort Chadbourne.

He was a career soldier. Born in Virginia in 1792, he had served in the military some 40 years before being sent to the western frontier. From John

Garland's many letters it is obvious this was not something he felt was advantageous to his illustrious career of the past. Not at any time does he write anything favorable about his time in this desolate country. Most of his letters rant and rave at the conditions, the lack of man power, and the "gross mismanagement somewhere." His words speak volumes. "I had hoped to be placed in a position which would enable me to work some good for the public service, but from the views entertained by the Commanding General of the Department, there is little or no prospect of my being able to accomplish any thing worthy of notice."[8] He cannot communicate with the Indians because they will not find him an interpreter, and he doesn't want the divisions separated, because he is from the old school where there is safety in numbers.

Here was a worn soldier, unhappy with finding himself stuck in the middle of nowhere, taking orders from a Headquarters he did not believe knew as much as he did. His disappointments, his anger, his tiredness from years of military duty showed in every word he put to paper.

In a letter to Major George Deas, Assistant Adjutant General in San Antonio, Texas, Garland wrote, "It had been a mistake to think that even half a regiment could be sheltered on the North Concho. There was not enough timber for building purposes, and what was there, was bad quality and ill shaped."

Garland began an immediate search for a better location. At the suggestion of a competent guide, John Conner[9], he went as far down as the crossing of the Colorado River, but deemed it too far east to suit the views of the General Commanding the Department.

As far back as the 1836, when Texas was an independent republic, the Delaware Indians were used as guides. John Conner was one of these men. He was often employed by the U. S. Government to work as a scout or interpreter for the military. Most guides were highly paid and many, such as Conner, were able to achieve land grants for their work, as Conner did some years later in Young County, Texas.

On Garland's return route from Camp McKavett, his attention was drawn to the many advantages at Kickapoo Springs, located 40 miles east of Camp Johnston. He felt there was an abundance of building materials including wood and stone, along with sufficient water to sustain an Army. Also, being in a direct line from Forts McKavett to Phantom Hill was perfect to his equation. He wrote, "It is my intention to press the examination of the country further north and west, but with little hopes of any other benefit than that to be desired from a better knowledge of the country."

His next directive was between Fort Phantom Hill and Camp Johnston. His letters to Headquarters, 8th U. S. Infantry, belittled many of the areas suggested for the Fort's placement in this region. His idea was still drawn to Kickapoo Springs, and to unite both wings of the 8th U. S. Infantry, at one location.

"I have been taught to know by long experience, that a force concentrated in the Indian Country sufficiently numerous to carry conviction to the minds of the Indians, that punishment is at hand and ready to be applied when occasion requires, will do more towards repressing hostilities, and preserving order on the frontier than a dozen posts occupied by small garrisons.

"It will also be found exceedingly beneficial to have some understanding between the military authorities and the Superintendent of Indian Affairs with several tribes of Indians as to the persons who shall be recognized as chiefs, with the further understanding that only those thus recognized will be counseled with at all. This will give confidence and authority to the Chiefs who in the present state of affairs have none. The rootless young men now go from one Independent Chief to another whenever whim or caprice tempts to do so.

"I have had talks with Sanaco, Buffalo Hump, Ketumpsee, and some others and find them jealous of each other. They are all agreed however in their determination to hang about the advanced posts for the double motive of protection and fear of starvation.

"I hope the General commanding the department will give these suggestions due consideration for much of our comfort, aside from public interest depends upon it."[10]

Although a new permanent site had yet to be found, in July 1852, Garland requisitioned Headquarters for a quantity of shingles and lumber for quarters needed for the right wing and Headquarters of the 8th U.S. Infantry. "The estimate is based upon the regulation allowance of quarters, and men, and what is commonly known as two pens and a passage with piazza on two sides."

Garland also requested an interpreter. "The Comanches are somewhat numerous in this vicinity and I am so poorly off for an interpreter that I can have no understanding with them. The Indians speak bad Spanish, and Sam Cherry[11] my guide still worse. In this dilemma I wish to get the services of John Conner for a few days. This is even more necessary as I have taken a Mexican boy from one of Sanaco's band who with five others was made prisoners a few months since. The Comanches wish to have some understanding with me in relation to these prisoners, but no one here is sufficiently conversant with their language to explain what I wish to say. Conner will not I suppose object to come over as his horse is here and he may get some clue to the other lost animals."[12]

Throughout July and August Garland remained persistent in his protest. The country up the North Concho was wholly unsuitable for a post; the timber was scarce; the hills barren; and due to heavy rains his excursions had been hampered north across the Colorado River. The area had already been visited by Captain Arthur Tracy Lee[13] to within thirty miles of the clear fork of the Brazos River. He agreed with Garland, and thought it was unsuitable for a fort as well.

September 10, 1852, a letter to the Brigadier General, 8th Department, San Antonio states, "The report of Captain Arthur Tracy Lee marked "A" was so very discouraging that in making the examination required of me, I put off for the last that section of the country which he had examined. My attention was however, strongly attracted to this particular point by the representatives of the Guide Sam Cherry, who I sent through to the post at Phantom Hill, and therefore determined to send the Regimental Quartermaster to make a thorough examination of it.

"I am exceedingly annoyed at the discrepancy in these reports but relying upon the better judgment of Lt. Holloway, feel satisfied that this statement by Cherry can be depended upon.

"The guide informs me that the place examined by Lt. Holloway[14] is not over sixty miles from Phantom Hill, thus, then if selected will throw the two wings of the regiment a hundred miles a part, and will add two days additional hauling for the trains beyond Camp Johnston.

"When it is taken into consideration that one band of Indians only occupies the country between the Concho and Phantom Hill and that several bands occupy the branches of the Concho, I am still of the opinion that the Kickapoo is the most eligible position in a military point of view, for the location of troops. It is not more than twenty miles further from the junction of the North with the main Concho than is Oak Creek and the expenses of constructing quarters at the latter would include an expense more than double that of the former."[15]

Garland's tirades go unheeded. At the preference of Department Commander Persifor F. Smith, on October 29, 1852, Fort Chadbourne was established. Companies A & K, Commanded by Fort Chadbourne's first commander, Captain John Beardsley[16] of the 8th U. S. Infantry, rode into an area some 35 miles northeast of Camp Johnston. It was located on Oak Creek in the northeast corner of present day Coke County. Company's I, G, and C would join over the next few weeks, along with many great and well known military officers to be determined in the future, such as, James Longstreet, George

Pickett, Robert E. Lee, John Bell Hood, Miles Keogh, and Earl Van Dorn.

At the time of establishment it was noted that Colonel John Garland was in San Antonio. A January 1853 post return states, "Colonel John Garland, 8th U. S. Infantry was released from arrest at San Antonio in December 1852, and joined and assumed command of Fort Chadbourne on January 10, 1853 when he relieved Captain Beardsley."

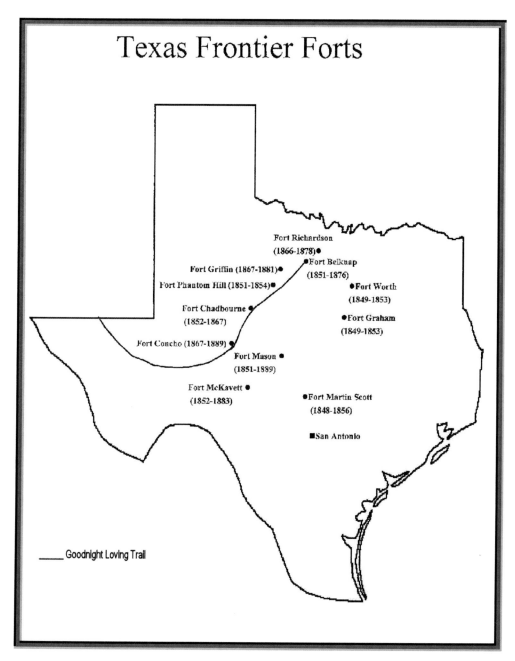

Texas Frontier Forts

Fort Richardson (1866-1878)

Fort Belknap (1851-1876)

Fort Griffin (1867-1881)

Fort Worth (1849-1853)

Fort Phantom Hill (1851-1854)

Fort Chadbourne (1852-1867)

Fort Graham (1849-1853)

Fort Concho (1867-1889)

Fort Mason (1851-1889)

Fort McKavett (1852-1883)

Fort Martin Scott (1848-1856)

San Antonio

——— Goodnight Loving Trail

Fig: 1

15

Chapter 11

Establish Fort Chadbourne

How did one begin such an enormous undertaking as building a fort in the middle of nowhere 150 years ago? As for Fort Chadbourne, the site was chosen because of its close proximity to not just water, but to a vast supply of building materials, such as stone and timber.

On arrival to the camp the Quartermaster, 1st Lt. Edmunds B. Holloway, hired a citizen master carpenter for $60.00 per month and a daily ration, along with a stone mason at $40.00 per month and also a ration. This was a practice long used by the military to hire civilians to do much of the manual labor at these forts.[17] Many of these men, especially the stone masons, were German immigrants from the Fredericksburg area of Texas.

New Post Commander, John Beardsley, also requested permission from Headquarters to employ men of the mounted portion of the command to assist in building the garrison.

Records indicate that the first structure to be built at Fort Chadbourne was the hospital. On March 1, 1853, the hospital, sixty feet by twenty feet, was listed as close to completion. Approximately ten days from that date only shingles were needed to make the hospital habitable.

Even though the hospital was the first building to be erected, it was never entirely finished. Throughout the years each and every report suggested window glass was needed for the windows. In addition, it was requested that a wood floor should also be added to make this a healthier environment for the sick. In the fifteen years it was used as a hospital, these features were never completed. Archeological investigations done in 2009, and 2010, confirmed these earlier reports.

It would normally take four men to rive out and shave five hundred shingles in a day if done on site. Then they would hardly be fit to cover a structure such as the hospital. Colonel John Garland requisitioned for these to be brought in from Fort Martin Scott; adding that the "shabby shingles on hand could perhaps be used to cover a store house of 100 x 20 feet; other than that they were almost worthless."[18]   A lack of man power was another quandary. Eight men were sent to the San Saba area to make shingles. Headquarters ordered an additional guard of four men be sent to Fort Martin Scott further depleting the number. After filling the requisitions for work in the Quartermasters Department, and other necessary details, there were scarcely enough men left to keep up a guard of nine men at the post.

Another great drawback arose from the large number of soldiers employed as teamsters in the service. In Garland's opinion these men when returned to their companies were generally deficient in their arms, ragged, filthy, and almost lawless.[19]

Even though, building continued throughout the next year. In July, 1st Lt. Holloway, Quartermaster, requisitioned the Department of Texas, Headquarters, for twelve pick axes, and it was approved. A reconnaissance was dispatched to examine the countryside within 20 miles of the post; to ascertain the quantity of timber capable of being used for building purposes, and if that timber could be obtained by labor of the troops at Fort Chadbourne.

From this exploration it was determined that post oak was the only timber found in any quantity. Its adaptation for building purposes was unfit for anything but rafters, joists, sleepers, and plates.

On August 13, 1853, an estimate for lumber required to finish Fort Chadbourne was submitted by Lt. Colonel Washington Seawell[20], 8th U. S. Infantry, to Headquarters.[21]

Flooring: (all items listed in square feet)

5 sets of company quarters	12,000
Quarters of N.C.S. & Band	1,560
Guard House	520
Commanding Officer, Quartermaster Office, & Court Room	1,674
Officers Quarter (includes 12' hall to each set of quarters)	17,662
Piazzas to Officers Quarters front and read	20,520
Piazzas to Hospital	<u>1,706</u>
Total Flooring Required	55,642

Doors and Window Sash:

156 Doors	5,408
Window Sash	<u>2,000</u>
Total	7,408

Laths:

Laths for lathing officers, commanding & Qrt Master   19,336

Roofing square feet:

Company Quarters 4	10,400
Quarters for N. C. S. & Band	1,680
Piazzas for 5 sets Company Quarters (front only)	5,500
Piazzas for N. C. S. & Band	715
Guard House	1,216
Piazza to same (front only)	352
Commanding Officer, Quartermaster, & Court Room	2,120
Piazzas to same (front only)	583
Officer's Quarters	16,270
Piazzas to same front and rear	13,870
Piazzas to Hospital	1,430
Magazine	288
Total	54,424
Wall Plate	3,172
Beams	2,685

Sleepers	10,300
Joists	10,300
Rafters	15,906
Door & Window Frames	6,446
Sheathing	54,424

That same month Lt. Colonel W. G Freeman[22], Assistant Adjutant General, visited Fort Chadbourne, to inspect the progress of the new Fort. The Freeman report has long been used as a source of reference when referring to the initial construction of these early military posts, and the personnel stationed there. He showed Fort Chadbourne situated in latitude 32° 02' North, longitude 100°14' West, about 2,100 feet above the sea, within a short distance of Oak Creek. Today if you use a global positioning system, and stand at the flag pole, in the center of the parade ground, your coordinates are exactly the same.

He noted with the exception of two or three crude jacal huts, the whole command was in tents. Only the hospital, one set of Company Quarters, and the storehouse were under roof. Shingles were brought in from the San Saba and cut by the troops.

Earlier in the year, the hospital and a storeroom were the only mention of buildings being erected. So apparently from March until Freeman visited in August a Company Quarters had been built and added to the list.

The storehouse used by the Quartermaster was hewn logs, one hundred feet long by eighteen feet wide. It was dry and secure, and provisions kept well. Average monthly disbursements were five hundred and fifty dollars. Approximately eighty of the soldiers were listed on extra duty, which Freeman noted later caused a problem in the ranks.

The hospital, a stone building, was well supplied with bedding and necessaries. The assistant surgeon considered the position entirely healthy, other than the occasional fever. What sickness there was seemed to stem from carelessness of the men, rather than any local cause or epidemic.

Freeman's observations of the troops at Fort Chadbourne implied they were in late pattern uniforms, and sited the supply for dress uniforms were not sufficient. The men were armed with Harper's Ferry muskets, percussion lock, Pattern 1845. There were twenty-four horses, some serviceable, some not.

Thirty soldiers were in possession of Maynard's primer muskets, 1850 models, but the soldiers complained these would not stand up to dampness.

Freeman noted there was a great need not only at Fort Chadbourne, but the other forts as well, for more superior quality non-commissioned officers in order to train the recruits. Although, his observation of troops was decent, he remarked that the number of extra duty men taken from their workshops, and grouped into the ranks for this occasion showed greatly. The men were easily spotted due to their soiled clothes, ungainly attitudes when at halt, and their unsteadiness of gait in marching.

On other occasions, Colonel John Garland had made almost the same statement, "When the soldiers are taken out of rank, and used as teamsters, their discipline falters, and they revert back to sloppy and disorderly soldiers." It was apparent that this was forever a challenge among the early days of these frontier forts, especially during the construction stage.

Freeman bestowed praise on the Fort Chadbourne band, exclaiming it was the finest in Texas. He added, its presence gave an interest and martial aspect to the performance of duty at the post.

His inspection of the sustenance department found on hand four hundred and sixty-four bushels of corn, and two hundred tons of hay. The corn was furnished from the depot in San Antonio, Texas, and cost approximately one dollar and fifty cents per bushel. There appeared to be enough provisions on hand for one month. Beef was served six days out of ten. The average cost of a ration per person was twenty and one half cents.

The hay, on the other hand was by contract at nine dollars and ninety six cents per ton. Although Freeman earlier accounted for twenty four horses, he later noted that approximately one hundred animals were foraged at the post monthly. This included sixty-six mules for the seven wagons in inventory, along with another ten animals not necessarily accounted for in this report.

In conclusion of his inspection he listed the Headquarters, along with five companies (A,C,G,I,K) of the 8th U. S. Infantry stationed here. Lt. Colonel Washington Seawell was presently in command.

Troops reviewed and inspected were:

Field and Staff: Lt. Col. Washington Seawell, 1st Lt. Edmunds B. Holloway-Regimental Quartermaster,

1st Lt. Thomas G. Pitcher-Adjutant, Eben Swift-Assistant Surgeon, and 17 men of non-commissioned staff and band.

Company A: 1st Lt. L. B. Wood and 40 men, 1st Lt. J.G.S. Snelling on sick report.

Company C: 2nd Lt. Malacthon Smith, 2nd Lt. Arthur P. Bagby and 28 men.

Company G: 2nd Lt. Richard Irving Dodge and 42 men

Company I: 1st Lt. George E. Pickett and 38 men.

Company K: Captain John Beardsley, 2nd Lt. James McIntosh and 41 men

Absent:

Field Officers: Colonel John Garland, Commanding 8th Department of Texas.

Company A: Captain Larkin Smith at Military Asylum, Washington D. C. since 1851, 2nd Lt. G. C. Barber in Subsistence Department at Indianola, 2nd Lt. P. Stockton on 20 days leave.

Company C: Captain Arthur Tracy Lee on leave of absence, 1st Lt. C. G. Merchant absent sick since 1849.

Company G: Captain J. Selden absent sick since 1847, 1st Lt. T. Fink in Quartermasters Department at Fort Martin Scott.

Company I: Captain James Longstreet on leave of absence, 2nd Lt. F. M Follett serving at Fort McKavett.

Chapter III
Dealing with Indians

It was during this summer that Indian Agent Robert Simpson Neighbors arrived at Fort Chadbourne to meet with Chiefs Sanaco, Buffalo Hump, Ketumse, Yellow Wolf, and others. On his arrival, August 24, 1853, he found the whole southern band of Comanches at the Fort, and spent ten days counseling with them in furthering plans to place them on reservations.[23]

Neighbors had long collaborated with the United States Government, Department of Texas, and the Indian tribes located in Texas. As early as the 1840's, he had negotiated for a diplomatic remedy to the situation in hopes of finding a peaceful outcome for the Indians and the white man to reside together. He labored for years to place the Indians on a reservation. The idea was to tame their wild nature, and in return bring to them civilization.

He presented a five point program... a: extinguish the Indian claim to as much as was needed for the immediate settlement of the whites; b: acquire enough land from Texas for a permanent settlement of the Indians of this state; c: extend the intercourse laws of the United States which regulated relations between Indians and whites; d: prohibit the sale of liquor to the Indians; and e: establish a general agency with at least three sub agencies to minister to the Comanches, Apaches, and establish military post to assist the agencies under these laws and treaties.

In 1851, Neighbors was elected to the Texas legislature, and served on the Committee on Indian Affairs in the House of Representatives through 1853. There, he helped pass a resolution to enter into negotiations with the United States Government to establish an Indian Territory in the northern part of the state.

In 1854, Neighbors and Captain Randolph Marcy met at Fort Belknap, and proceeded to examine areas for the Indian reserves in present day Throckmorton and Young counties. The Comanche reserve consisted of four leagues of land on the Clear Fork of the Brazos River. There was other land set aside and several Texas tribes considered for other reservations, but this book mainly touches on the Comanches, and occasionally the Kiowa, because they were the bands most associated with the area of Fort Chadbourne.

As Neighbors was making a trip in the area late 1854, through Fort Chadbourne on his way to Fort Belknap, he learned that a campaign under Captain W. J. Newton, at Fort Chadbourne, was assembled. Newton had made it plain that there would be no distinction made between hostile and friendly Indians. All Indians would be pursued regardless.

Neighbors and Marcy discovered acquiring land for the reservations was not a problem, but now transferring the Indians would be. News of the campaign in early 1855, to pursue any and all Indians as hostile, led Sanaco and the southern band of Comanches in this area to break camp and head north to the Red River area, before Neighbors could get them settled. It is believed that the Fort Chadbourne post trader John Leyendecker[24] was the gentleman responsible for issuing this alarm to Sanaco and the other Chiefs concerning the expedition and their extermination. Only Chief Ketumse and his band, unbelieving of the rumor, remained and were agreeable to the move. Later they were placed on the reservation.[25]

Neighbors hearing this contacted Texas Governor Pease concerning the expedition. He asked the Governor to speak with Brevet General Persifor Smith, Department of Texas, and arrange for orders to be issued that would suspend hostilities against the friendly Indians until they could be colonized.

Neighbors left for Washington D. C., to confer about the placements of the reservations, and gave Agent Howard special instructions to follow in his absence. Howard was to go to Fort Chadbourne and cooperate with Captain Newton, 2nd U. S. Dragoons, in a campaign against the northern and middle bands of the Comanches. Howard was told in no uncertain terms that the southern Comanches, who were the bands near Fort Chadbourne, and were now a concern to Neighbors, were not to be threatened. Agent Howard failed to carry out these orders.

Three companies of the Texas Mounted Volunteers, Company's A, D, and F, arrived at the post, and were mustered into service on December 23, 1854, to aid the 2nd U. S. Dragoons, in a campaign against the Comanches. Captain W. J. Newton, first in command of the expedition, relinquished his command to Captain Patrick Calhoun, who at this time was Post Commander. These Texas Volunteers would remain in service of the United States for three months until they were mustered out on March 23, 1855.[26]

Per Headquarters, Department of Texas, the expedition did not leave the post until it was furnished with everything necessary. Requisitions for supplies were filled through the San Antonio Depot without waiting for the approval of the Department Commander.

Before the expedition from Fort Chadbourne left, the southern band of Comanches, having heard of the expedition, had already scattered north. Although the soldiers and volunteers departed from Fort Chadbourne as ordered, there was no confrontation with the Comanche's.

It was Neighbors hope that the damage done to the southern Comanches, simply by word of this expedition, could be repaired and they would settle down, and be moved to the reservations without further calamity.

But in 1856, in temporary command of the Department of Texas, Colonel Albert Sidney Johnston notified the Secretary of War that the Indian depredations continued, and in fact, the Indians had grown more aggressive.

On May 27, 1856, Privates Robins Cady and John Haines, Company F, U. S. 1st U. S. Infantry, stationed at Fort Chadbourne, were killed by Indians while returning with the mail from Fort McKavett. Major Seth Eastman, then commanding Fort Chadbourne, described the location of the attack at or near a water hole about nine miles south of the Colorado River, and on the road that led from Fort Chadbourne to Fort Mason, at approximately 3:00 p.m.. A scouting party was sent out on June 1, 1856, and on that day one body was found and recovered. The body was mutilated with four arrows to its side, along with a shirt and trousers, and one letter found near by. As of the June 4th report from Eastman, the scouting party was continuing to search for the other body, and to ascertain if any Indians were killed in the attack. Scouts reported that the Indians appeared to be traveling in a southwest direction.[27]

Since the mail carriers were well armed with Colt pistols, and Yager rifles, in all probability, some Indians were killed or wounded. With information received from scouts, along with the Superintendent of the Indian Department of Texas, it was believed the increase of robberies and murders on the frontier were being done by Sanaco's band, in association with the northern Comanches.

On June 7, 1856, approximately twenty Comanches, both male and female, rode into Fort Chadbourne requesting to talk to the Commander, Major Seth Eastman. The fact that one Indian had in his possession what appeared to be the mail carriers gun, along with pieces and parts of mail addressed to the Fort, it led Lt. C. W. Thomas to believe these were indeed the Comanches that had burned, tortured, and killed Privates Cady and Haines a few days earlier.

Lt. Thomas arranged for the Indians to council with Captain Eastman while he drilled his Company near by with loaded rifles. After a few minutes, he faced his Company towards the group of Indians, and demanded their surrender. Immediately a fight ensued, and seven Indians were killed, and most likely all of those who escaped were wounded. Their Chief ran into Captain Eastman's house and barred the door. From all indications, and the information available at Fort Chadbourne today in relation to the officer's quarters and the hand dug well, Eastman's quarters appears to be the one referred to in present day as the "Fountain House"[28].

Inside the house the Chief was armed with a rifle and revolver. He refused to surrender and fired through the door at any noise, or person, that approached from the outside.

Lt. Thomas, tired of trying to kill the Chief by guesswork, ordered his men to bring a rail and ram the door down. As the door went down, Lt. Thomas leapt into the room. The Chief was squatted down behind a desk, and as he rose to fire at him. Thomas brought him down with a single shot through the head.[29]

The letter dated, June 8, 1856, from Commander Eastman, recounts that on that date the Express Riders remains were buried at Fort Chadbourne, along with the seven Indians that were killed within the post.

In correspondence from Assistant Adjutant General D. C. Buell, Headquarters, Department of

Texas, he commended Captain Eastman in his handling of the affair, which resulted in the killing of the seven Indians. He relayed to the Commander that he had the Departments utmost approval for the procedures he and his men had carried out.

Buell further emphasized that all Indians in Texas that were not settled on the reserve and under control, were to be regarded as hostiles, and be pursued and attacked, whenever and wherever, they could be found. Only the Shawnees, and Delaware's, were to be an exception to the rule, for he found their conduct undisputed.[30]

Following the correspondence between Buell and Eastman, orders were provided from Department of Texas, Commander Persifor F. Smith, to Lt. Colonel Robert E. Lee at Camp Cooper. He was ordered to assemble two cavalry companies of forty men per company, take thirty days provisions, two tents per company for the sick, hire guides and pack mules, and set off for Fort Chadbourne. This was Lee's first independent combat command. After marching the hundred miles to the Fort, Lee merged his command with two more cavalry companies. These commanded by Major Earl Van Dorn, and Captain Theodore

O'Hara. Lee was also urged to consult with Indian Agent Neighbors as to probable locations of Indians. Jim Shaw[31] along with fifteen other Delaware trailers were to scout for him.

The expedition targeted any and all Indians who still carried on depredations against the settlements. This applied mostly to Sanaco's band, but the orders applied equally to any other Indians in the region who were engaged in mischievous ways, and harmful to the settlements of Texas. Their continued rejection to peaceably settle on the reservations was proof of their unfriendliness, and under order of the Department Commander they should be pursued to the utmost limit the command would permit. They should be treated with rigorous hostility wherever they could be found.

On June 18, 1856, Lt. Colonel Lee rendezvoused at Fort Chadbourne, with Companies A and F from Camp Cooper, and B and G from Fort Mason. With the four companies of cavalry, supply wagons, guides and interpreters, they rode northwest from Chadbourne toward the headwaters of the branches of the Brazos, and Colorado Rivers. Earlier accounts had reported a large number of Chief Sanaco's band gathered there, not far from Fort Chadbourne.

The soldiers were some four days ride from the post before any visible signs of Indians were located. They happened upon several abandoned camp sites, along with fresh trails, but no Indians were found. The summer heat was taking its toll on the men, so Lee sent several men back to Fort Chadbourne calling for reinforcements to continue his search.

After a month with no new discoveries, Lee divided his command into three units in order to cover a greater territory. Lee himself commanded one group, Van Dorn and O'Hara the others. In all only Van Dorn's group was fruitful. Van Dorn's men saw smoke signals, which suggested the presence of an Indian camp near by. Expecting to find a large number, he was surprised when only three Comanche warriors, and one Indian woman, were present in the camp. A fight broke out, and two warriors were killed, while the other mounted his horse and got away. They then captured the woman along with twelve horses. Expecting to find a larger band, Van Dorn spread out his troops, but it was in vain. All trails led to Mexico, and after some thousand miles of travel the expedition was called off, and Van Dorn, Lee, O'Hara, and their troops returned to Camp Cooper. Van Dorn departed Camp Cooper a few weeks later on July 28, 1856, to set up a new military establishment to be known as Camp Colorado.[32]

In late 1856, Colonel Albert Sidney Johnston at this time Colonel, 2nd U. S. Cavalry, now Commanding Department Headquarters, requested Colonel Samuel Cooper, Adjutant General of the Army, to rethink the feasibility of issuing permits to Indians by Indian Agents, or by Commanding Officers, at the various posts. He reasoned that this was a great embarrassment to his operations, as his troops had been told that any Indian away from the reservation was to be considered hostile. By distributing these permits, and allowing these Indians to come into this area of Texas to hunt was not a good practice, and Johnston felt it should be discontinued immediately. He suggested the thirty-third parallel of latitude now being used as a boundary line be changed. The Red River, which was a well known geographical location could be used as the boundary line which everyone would recognize.[33]

In the meantime, Captain John H. King, Company I, 1st U. S. Infantry, now commanding Fort Chadbourne, sent a letter to Headquarters requesting his men be sent horses. Captain John Withers, Assistant Adjutant General responded by saying Captain King was not authorized to purchase horses for mounting the infantry, but that he could use public mules for mounting his men when necessary.

It is interesting the military stationed infantry, instead of cavalry units, at Fort Chadbourne and other military posts across the frontier. Expecting these soldiers to chase and corral Indians across these wide open spaces without the use of horses, was somewhat ridiculous. Then, when requesting mounts for their men, Headquarters replied mules could be used to pursue hostile Indians who were riding some of the fastest ponies scattered all across Texas.

Withers did provide some relief though by directing Major George H. Thomas, who at that time was Commanding Camp Cooper, to send a detachment of the 2nd U. S. Cavalry to Fort Chadbourne. It consisted of one Sergeant, one Corporal, and thirteen Privates, who were to report to King for duty at Fort Chadbourne and remain there until June. He also authorized King to employ a guide whenever he deemed necessary. [34]

On April 7, 1857, detachments from Companies E and H, 2nd U. S. Cavalry from Camp Cooper, met at Fort Chadbourne, and they immediately went out on a scout. They remained under Fort Chadbourne command until May 26th, when they returned to Camp Cooper with no action reported.

It was during this time that Brevet Major General David E. Twiggs recommended the creation of the Texas Mounted Volunteers. The Texas Legislature urged the U. S. Congress to pass a law equipping a regiment of Texas volunteers, for a minimum of twelve months of service. In January 1858, the bill passed. It authorized the state government of Texas to call one hundred rangers to aid in the protection of the frontier, and appropriated seventy thousand dollars to be used towards that objective.

Captain John Ford, Texas Mounted Volunteers, assisted the federal troops, and Headquarters, Department of Texas. Twiggs ordered the commanding officers at all posts, including Fort Chadbourne, to cooperate with Ford's troops. As early as February, Ford and his troops were on an expedition of the Red and Brazos Rivers. The Texas forces, seeking an end to the Indian depredations across the frontier of Texas, attacked a Comanche camp in May killing seventy-six Indian warriors.

After seeing some progress, Twiggs decided he liked this sort of policy. He felt after ten long years of being on the defensive it was time for the troops to ride into Indian Territory to assist the rangers, and give the Indians a dose of their own medicine. He hoped the Indians would then leave Texas alone!

A few months later a detachment of the 1st U. S. Infantry, under the command of Captain Van Dorn, left Fort Belknap, crossed into the area of the Red River, and attacked a Comanche encampment, killing fifty-five warriors.

Although until 1859, great strides were made, and progress was seen on the reservations, other Comanche tribes, including Sanaco's group continued their raids in Texas. Settlers believing it was the reservation Indians that were attacking the frontier, led to the killing of many Indians caught off the reservation, along with illegal acts carried out on the reserves themselves. This eventually led Neighbors to move the reservations from Texas to reservations in the Washita Valley of Indian Territory in present day Oklahoma.

In September of 1859, Robert Simpson Neighbors, while near Fort Belknap, was shot in the back and killed by a man named Edward Cornett. Some believed it was a direct occurrence of his on going efforts to protect the Indians.

Chapter IV

A. B. Gray

The new year of 1854 brought visitor's to the Fort. Andrew Belcher Gray's expedition for the purpose of examining the 32nd parallel, and a prospective railroad between San Antonio and San Diego, arrived at the post. All expenses were paid by Texas Western Railroad Company. Their route followed northward by way of Fredericksburg, Texas and Fort Mason, crossing the Guadeloupe, Piedernallis, Llano, San Saba, and Concho Rivers, then the west fork of the Colorado River and arriving at Fort Chadbourne on January 13, 1854.

After a couple of days rest the men traveling with Colonel Gray departed. Gray and Peter Rainsford Brady, an associate surveyor, remained behind to partake in the further hospitality of Lt. James M. Hawes[35], 2nd U. S. Dragoons. He was an old acquaintance of Colonel Gray's, and now in Command of Fort Chadbourne.

Hawes had the reputation of being not only gregarious, but a good mixer of milk punch. Milk punch, made with bourbon and milk, was a popular drink of the time much like our eggnog of today. Occasionally the drink was flavored with other ingredients such as vanilla or nutmeg.

After passing the morning with their old friend, Gray and Brady saddled up and left Fort Chadbourne around noon. Lt. Hawes insisted upon filling their canteens with his concoction of the alcohol laced punch. His friends were much appreciative for his generosity.

They had expected to catch up with the rest of their party by evening, but things didn't go as planned. This was the Texas frontier!

The day was unusually warm for January, with a touch of spring in the air. The temperature had climbed to a pleasant 70 degrees. But as they rode along, around mid afternoon they could see a large bank of dark clouds in the north. Weather could change quickly in West Texas, and they figured things were a fixin' to change in a big way. As the clouds moved closer, a piercing cold wind blew in and the temperature plunged until it reached a frigid 3 degrees, a drop of 67 degrees in only a few hours time.

They were in an area with no trees, flat barren land, nothing for shelter, and they had not managed to catch up with the rest of their group. They had no choice but to dismount and pass the long January night with no wood for a fire, and nothing to eat. Even their animals were shivering. They bundled up as best they could, and passed the long freezing night with a cold wind howling around them. The milk punch, even though laced with alcohol, was now frozen solid in their canteens. They could not even enjoy that. At daybreak they mounted up hoping to find their group as quickly as possible. The night had been so cold that even one of the forks of the Concho River was frozen over solid; so solid their mules could walk on it. The only thing they had for sustenance was the punch, so they hunted up some sticks and whittled them down to get to the milky drink frozen inside their canteens. They finally enjoyed what they called a nourishing and slightly stimulating breakfast.

As the morning wore on, riding along the trail they found the location where their party had camped for the night, and had apparently enjoyed a warm fire and hot meal. They traveled approximately twelve more miles before finally overtaking the other members of the expedition.[36]

There was now no evidence of the milk punch. Miles back it had melted and miraculously disappeared down their throats. The other members of the group probably wondered why, after these two had spent a night almost freezing to death, they were in such a light hearted and jovial mood!

For the next few months life was relatively quiet at the post. Dr. Eben Swift, Assistant Surgeon reported the post had been very healthy during the quarter. In April, due to a recent flurry of Indian raids, General Persifor Smith, Headquarters, Department of Texas ordered all disposable forces at Forts Inge, McKavett, and Chadbourne to take a detachment of fifteen men and patrol the country from the Nueces to Fort Chadbourne.

On June 9th, a terrible storm blew through and hailstones were said to drift up to a depth of six to eight feet deep in the bed of Oak Creek. The soldiers were said to have gathered some twenty wagon loads of the hailstones. Severe storms plagued the Fort for the next two weeks. Not only was the weather volatile that summer, but several months later they were inundated with grasshoppers. It took the pest three days to move through. They were so dense they appeared as a snowstorm. Seldom was life pleasant for these soldiers stationed on the frontier.[37]

Although the indications point to a rainy and stormy summer, 2nd Lt. George Steuart found it hot and lonely. In a letter to his sister in Baltimore he told her, "there is so few soldiers here right now that there is hardly any need for so many officers." He added, with nothing to do here he thought he should be paid more, or at least be given more leave of absence. He was cut off from all society, comforts, and the enjoyments of a civilized life. If he could get leave in the fall or winter, he would be headed home to see her.

He joked with her about joining the Comanches. They had hung around the post all summer, but it had helped to keep things lively. He lent his description of them to his sister back in Baltimore. She was probably captivated by his writings, and imagined the stories she'd heard and read about concerning the wild Indians. Now her dear brother lived among them.

Lt. Steuart described how the young squaws were dressed in blue and red, and the young men in red and blue blankets embroidered with beads. They had long braids of buffalo hair ornamented with silver. He said, "Just before they left the area there was word from Mexico that some of their warriors had been killed, and they all cut off their hair and horses tails. The squaws mutilated and cut their arms with knives. He noticed that the young men took care to disfigure themselves as little as possible. Chief Tiaquash, he explained, the one who is very smart and a friend of the whites, took care that his wife did not cut herself as much, or crop her hair."

It appeared Lt. Steuart enjoyed writing to his sister about the Indians and their helping to pass his boredom when they came into the post. But, he too thought, as Colonel Garland had earlier, that they were bothersome and beggars, especially the women.

In the book "The U. S. Army and the Texas Frontier Economy", Lt. Steuart was used as example as to how mail to most Texas forts should be addressed. The name and rank of the soldier should appear along with his regiment, and it was sent in care of the U. S. Quartermaster, in San Antonio. Eventually, it would make its way to the correct frontier forts along the route.

Lt. Steuart for instance wrote his sister Mary in Baltimore on August 16, 1854, and she received it on September 12, 1854, twenty-eight days later. His reply and her return reply both had envelopes, something unusual even five years prior. Both took a three cent stamp and were franked through New Orleans.

Springtime 1855 at Fort Chadbourne, brought Company F, of the U. S. 2nd U. S. Dragoons, along with ten new Sharps carbines. They were the latest and greatest weaponry for their time on the frontier, and issued to each Dragoon company. In September the post was reinforced with the arrival of the Adjutant, Regimental Quartermaster, non-commissioned staff, and band of the 2nd U. S. Dragoons, by Order No. 79, Headquarters, Department of Texas, along with three companies of Texas Mounted Volunteers in November.

Companies C, G, I, and K of the 8th U. S. Infantry were transferred from Fort Chadbourne via San Antonio. Company C to Ringgold Barracks near the Rio Grande, and Companies I and K to El Paso. Forty wagons were assigned to transport the one hundred and ninety eight men, leaving approximately fifty-nine men from Company A at the post.[38]

Chapter V

Military Burial

In the fall of 1854, and winter of 1855, there was increased Indian activity around the Fort. Before the Comanches and Kiowa's scattered in fear for their lives, Sanaco, one of the Comanche Chiefs was a frequent visitor. He would come into the Fort and to the officers skepticism Sanaco would ask them to write on a piece of paper the name of some article, such as "sugar". He would then carefully fold the paper and put it away. The next day he would seek out another officer and ask him to write something down, this time perhaps "coffee". He made the rounds of all the officers asking them to write down different items. They weren't sure what he was up to, but assumed he was making medicine of some kind. Several weeks later a messenger for Sanaco came into the fort with a piece of paper. On the paper was a list, such as sugar, coffee, flour, etc. The item list was signed by Sanaco.

He had diligently forged each of the officer's handwritings to perfection when scripting the items on the list. The officers could not distinguish their own handwriting from the forgeries.[39]

Besides the Comanche Chief Sanaco, Chief Satanta from the Kiowa tribe would camp near the fort, and he too would repeatedly come into the post. One officer's wife who resided at Fort Chadbourne during that time remembers Satanta on his splendid mount riding into the post, dressed in beautiful attire, carrying a shield ornamented with a tale of magnificent brown hair taken from a white woman's scalp.[40]

Years later Chief Satanta was arrested for his depredations and incarcerated at Huntsville, Texas. In October 1878, realizing there was no chance for freedom, Satanta, rather than spend his life in chains, jumped to his death from a second story landing. Some historians question that and suggest he was pushed.

During this time a regiment of the Texas troops was camped on the banks of Oak Creek near Fort Chadbourne. These men composed of Texas Rangers and Volunteers made up the "Army of Texas". They were often enlisted by the United States and served as scouts and escorts on many occasions. These troops were not part of the three companies that mustered into the forces later in October.

John Y. Rankin[41] was one of these mounted volunteers. A fellow ranger Bill Ragsdal <sic> had been feeling under the weather for several days, and the night before his passing, Rankin spent the night checking on his friend. At sunrise he and fellow rangers found Mr. Ragsdal <sic> unresponsive. Rankin sent for Dr. Swift at Fort Chadbourne, requesting his assistance as soon as possible. When Dr. Swift arrived, he pronounced Ragsdal <sic> dead. Mr. Rankin's diary is the only reference describing a burial at the post. It reads: "That evening Ragsdal <sic> was buried at Fort Chadbourne as an American soldier. The company went to the grave and in order, the corpse was carried on a cannon card, drawn by two

John Rankin

mules with the stars and stripes over the coffin, the brass band played a piece of music and a platoon of regular soldiers fired three rounds of blank cartridges over the grave. Service was read by Dr. Swift of the post and the grave closed. We have lost a good soldier, a kind and sincere friend, an exceptional mess mate. He has not an enemy in the whole company. May his soul rest in peace shall forever be my sincere prayer." The next day the Texas Rangers left the Fort.[42]

Albert Sidney Johnston served as paymaster to these frontier forts during this time period. After his district was enlarged to include Forts Belknap, Phantom Hill, Chadbourne, and McKavett this alone added another two hundred and fifty miles to his circuit. He accepted this job in hopes of promotion and his own Army command. But after five long years his wife Eliza wrote that Albert looked worn and thin, and she predicted he would not last long with this sort of life. He was continually exposed to exhausting heat in summer, frigid cold in winter; sleeping on hard ground, and being away from his wife and children. At times his son William Preston accompanied him, and this made both Eliza and Albert feel better. But, after five years riding the same trail six times a year, he expressed his misgivings to the paymaster general.

Paymasters such as Johnston traveled to these frontier posts with little protection, and were in care of several thousand dollars of Army money at a time. Numerous times over a period of two years, approximately four thousand dollars of the money vanished, and Johnston made up the loss out of his own savings. It was during one of these trips when his son Will was along. Will alleged to his father that a trusted Negro slave named John was perhaps the culprit. Will marked some of the coins, and later they were found in John's possession. John, in some way or other, had acquired a duplicate key to the strongbox and helped himself at random. John had been a close friend to Johnston, or so Johnston thought, so instead of having the slave whipped, he sold him for one thousand dollars to repay some of the debt. "Whipping will not restore what is lost, and it will not benefit the Negro, whom a lifetime of kind treatment has failed to make honest", said Johnston.[43]

Perchance it was the very same trip in March that Will Johnston spoke of in his journal, when he and his father arrived at Fort Chadbourne mid afternoon. They had looked over muster rolls, partook of a good dinner in the officer's mess, and spent the night in Captain Patrick Calhoun's quarters. They departed the next morning after paying the accounts.[44]

In June, by special Order No. 60, a readjustment of troops occurred. Fort Chadbourne received two Companies, D and F of the 1st U. S. Infantry from Fort Duncan, while the 2nd U. S. Dragoons now stationed at the post were disbursed to Fort Riley, Kansas. The new troops arrived on August 13, 1855. Captain Seth Eastman, 1st U. S. Infantry, relieved Captain Patrick Calhoun, 2nd U. S. Dragoons as Commander of Fort Chadbourne.

Arriving along with Eastman was 2nd Lt. Zenus Bliss. Lt. Bliss, a friend of Captain Calhoun gave him a beautiful Russian leather perfumery case before he left. It containing four cut glass bottles filled with perfume, and Calhoun was said to have kept it for many years.

Together Eastman and Bliss organized a lodge while at the Fort, called "Lone Star". Mr. E. D. Lane a sutler from Fort McKavett was the grand commander and delivered the lectures. This order was afterwards known as the "Sons of Malta".

The rest of 1855 was fairly quiet compared to the previous years. There continued to be Indian sightings, and several times scouting trips were sent out from the Fort. Lt. Bliss had an encounter one evening immediately following his arrival at Fort Chadbourne. Some Indians were seen in the garden, which was approximately one mile from the Fort, and Lt. Bliss along with his group of sixteen men proceeded to the garden. They searched through the night and since none of the men were familiar with the area, they spent most of the night lost. With the arrival of daylight, they found themselves within a half mile of the post. Of course they realized they had no chance of finding Indians in the dark, and if by chance they had happened upon one, Bliss said the Indians would probably have killed them, and escaped into the dark.[45]

Chapter VI

J.K.F. Mansfield

And A.G. Miller Reports

The Indians became bolder in their attacks on the settlers and soldiers, leaving the military no choice but to deal with the situation at hand.

Following the encounter with the Indians at Fort Chadbourne in July 1856 and the murder of the mail carriers, Captain Seth Eastman took a seven day leave of absence. Although he left on the 16th, he still had not returned at the time of an inspection performed by Colonel J. K. F. Mansfield.

Mansfield had however met Captain Eastman at Fort Mason on his way to Fort Chadbourne, and Eastman informed him he was sick and on leave.

Mansfield later reported that Eastman did appear quite ill and looked very feeble.

On July 27th and 28th 1856, the inspection at Fort Chadbourne was performed by Colonel Mansfield. His findings follow:

Field and Staff: Assistant Surgeon Elisha P. Langworthy and Ordnance Sergeant.

Company D, 1st U. S. Infantry: Captain Seth Eastman left post sick on seven day leave on the 16th of July for San Antonio, 1st Lt. T. A. Washington at the Military Academy since 1854, No 2nd Lts present, 4 Sergeants, 3 Corporals, 2 musicians, 48 men for duty, 7 extra duty, 6 sick, 1 confined, 1 at Headquarters, Department of Texas, 1 at Headquarter 1st U. S. Infantry, 9 on detached service. Total at command no officer and 80 men.

Company F, 1st U. S. Infantry: No Captain, 1st Lt. C. C. Gilbert[46] detached since April 1856, 2 Lt. C. W. Thomas acting Assistant Quartermaster since March 1856, 3 Sergeants, 4 Corporals, 2 musicians; 48 men for duty, 5 extra duty, 6 sick, 3 confined, and 9 on detached service. Total at command: 1 officer and 80 men.

Aggregate Command: 20 Officers and 160 men, 1 Assistant Surgeon, 1 Ordnance Sergeant.

Colonel Mansfield's inspection of Company D found the men residing in a shingled, stone building. At the time the stone building he spoke of would be one of the two barracks that were near completion on his visit. The mess room and kitchens located north of the barracks, consisted of logs covered with canvas. Company property was well stored and the canteens were in good shape. There were two laundresses. Company D had suffered three desertions in 1855 and one in 1856. Attached to the Company were eighty-two serviceable muskets, three rifles, three Colt pistols, two musician's swords, and ample ammunition in storage. They reported no iron bedsteads.

Company F's quarters were neat and of the same stone and shingled roof as Company D's. Mess room and kitchen were the same as Company D's, and found to be of the same log and canvas materials. Property was well stored, and there were four laundresses. They too had no iron bedsteads. There were seven desertions in 1855; none in 1856. Attached to the Company were seventy-eight muskets altered to the Maynard primer, but defective as they did not go off in the course of fire except two or three times during time trials. Mansfield noted that the springs were probably too weak, but there was suitable ammunition.

Following building inspections, the Companies were drilled, and they did not do as well as expected. D Company fired at a target 100 yards away, only hitting one out of eight. F Company faired better, but still not good with only one out of four.

There was no magazine at Fort Chadbourne. To this day no reference has been found to show there ever was one, but two twelve pound brass howitzers were attached to the post, and there were suitable ammunitions for them. However, the forges and howitzer carriages were in need of paint.

The hospital was under the control of Assistant Surgeon Elisha P. Langworthy and consisted of a stone building with shingles and canvas windows. The kitchen located west of the hospital was of logs with a canvas roof. There were ample supplies and unlike the enlisted men's barracks, the hospital had iron bedsteads. There was a good steward and matron present, along with fourteen sick in the building. Mansfield suggested that glass windows be allowed in the hospital, and condemned fourteen sheets, eight towels, eight pillow cases, and two pillow ticks. He suggested they be cut into bandages or rags.

The Fort Chadbourne Guard House and Prison were of logs with a canvas roof. There were four prisoners incarcerated on the day of inspection; two for drunkenness, and two for sleeping on post.

Lt. C. W. Thomas served as Quartermaster. It was well managed. Supplies were received from San Antonio except hay, which was purchased at seventeen dollars per ton. Corn was purchased at one dollar seventy cents per hundred locally.

Lumber was much needed for coffins. At inspection time, the dead were buried in coffins made of pieces of wood from the commissary, ordnance boxes, or old chests. Shingles were just as much in need, as was the lumber. Last but not least added to the list was a need for a horse cart.

The Quartermaster kept in his employ one clerk, four teamsters, two herdsmen, three express men, one carpenter, one blacksmith, six horses, thirty-nine mules, four wagons, and one ambulance. His accounts were in good order. The Quartermaster's office was located in a building also used for Adjutants and

Commissary office's, sharing with a store house once again built of logs and canvas.

The Granary, Harness Store, and Blacksmith Shop's were of the same materials, but the Carpenters Shop was made of canvas. The Bakery was a log hut, shingled, and had a good oven and bread. There was also an attempt at a large garden, but it had failed due to lack of rain. A good corral was listed along with sixty tons of hay on hand.

Officers were quartered in log buildings with canvas covers, except one, which was of stone and shingled. The unmarried officers had a mess.

The Commissary attended by Lt. Thomas had a good supply on hand, including fresh beef that could be had for ten cents a pound. Most of these items were again received from San Antonio, approximately a three day ride from the post.

Following up on Colonel Mansfield's suggestions, commanding officer at that time, 1st Lt. A. G. Miller, 1st U. S. Infantry wasted no time in contacting Major D. C. Buell, Assistant Adjutant General. He noted that stone could be easily procured on site, but lumber would need to be purchased in Fredericksburg, and transported to Fort Chadbourne by wagon.

Miller believed the guard house was in miserable condition, along with the two separate quarters where Lt. Thomas and Assistant Surgeon Langworthy now resided. These buildings had dirt floors and were in much need of repair before cold weather. His own quarters, listed as logs and shingles, was in no better shape, and one set of officers quarter's leaked so bad it could be considered worthless.

The hospital roof needed repairs too, along with adding sashes, and there was a desperate need for panes of glass in the windows. When the weather was cold and inclement the interior was almost in total darkness because canvas was used to cover the windows.

Miller and Mansfield both drew a sketch of the locations of buildings. Miller added proposed quarters to his map, hopefully looking to the future when the huts that most of them now resided in would be replaced with serviceable stone buildings. (See Fig. 2, Fig. 3)[47]

On August 7, 1856, 2nd Lt. C. W. Thomas, Quartermaster, Fort Chadbourne, requisitioned Colonel A. C. Myers, Chief Quartermaster for the following building materials with the approval of Post Commander, 1st Lt. A. G. Miller, 1st U. S. Infantry..

Officers Quarters:
- 35,000 Shingles
- 9,000 Feet Sheathing Boards
- 6,000 Feet Flooring
- 120 Rafters, 25 feet long
- 85 flooring joists, 25 feet long
- 20 Panel doors
- 25 Window Sashes
- 350 Panes of Window glass, 10"x12"

Guardhouse Repairs:
- 2,000 Shingles
- 10 Rafters
- 500 Feet Sheathing Boards

East Barracks Repairs:
- 18,000 Shingles
- 4,500 Feet Sheathing Boards
- 60 Rafters

Hospital Repairs:

- 12 Window Sashes
- 144 Panes of Glass

Building Quarters:

- 4 Keg Shingle Nails
- 1 Keg 8d Nails
- 1 Keg 10d Nails
- 1 Keg 12d Nails
- 30 Lbs Putty
- 2 Kegs White Lead
- 2 Gallons Oil for Paint

Upon the arrival of Lt. Thomas' list in San Antonio, Assistant Adjutant General Buell recommended to the Quartermaster General that the above supplies be provided, and added that providing suitable accommodations for the troops was a high priority of the War Department.[48]

Items requisitioned were not always building materials. Elisha P. Langworthy, the Assistant Surgeon at Fort Chadbourne for only a few months, also had to take care of the meteorological duties while stationed here.   Langworthy wrote to the Surgeon General in Washington, D. C. and requested that new floss silk be sent to him for use on the hygrometer, an instrument that measures humidity.   Apparently the one he had at the time was encrusted, rotten, and almost worthless.

Assistant Surgeon Langworthy sent monthly statements, and received copies of Assistant Surgeon Henderson's work relating to the medical examination of recruits.   He acknowledged the reception of a circular on the subject of neglect by Medical Officers, along with revised medical regulations.[49] Langworthy departed Fort Chadbourne for Fort McKavett in December 1856.

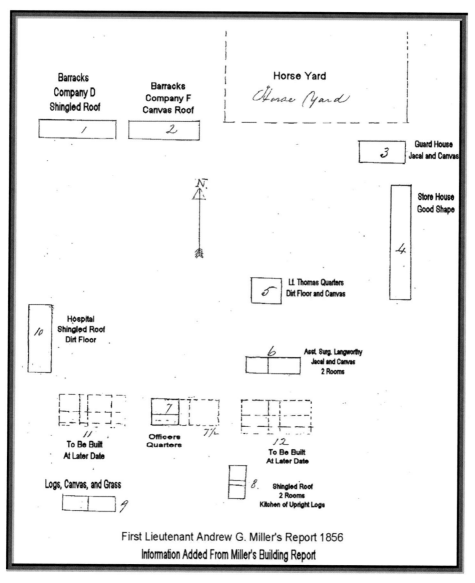

First Lieutenant Andrew G. Miller's Report 1856
Information Added From Miller's Building Report

Fig: 2

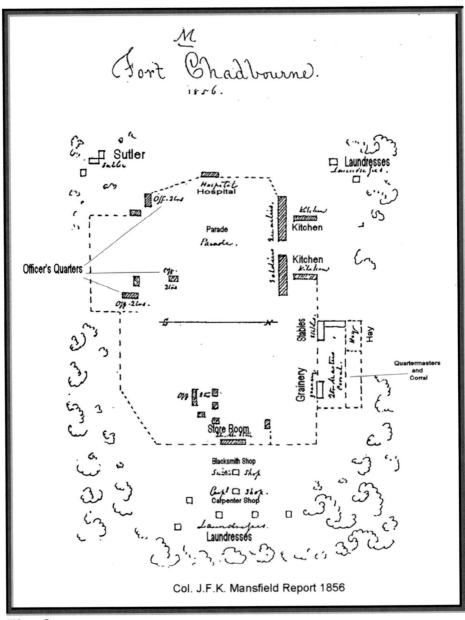

Col. J.F.K. Mansfield Report 1856

Fig. 3

Chapter VII

1ˢᵗ Lt. T. A. Washington
Takes Inventory

As the long summer days passed into fall and winter, Headquarters, Department of Texas, ordered a detachment of twenty men of the 2ⁿᵈ U. S. Cavalry sent from Camp Cooper to Fort Chadbourne to be used for scouting purposes.[50]

Also arriving at the post after a leave of absence was Fort Chadbourne's first recorded Chaplin and Schoolmaster, Reverend Tobias A. Michell, D. D., Protestant Episcopal Church. It was by General Orders No. 10, War Department, on September 1, 1856 that Fort Chadbourne was placed on the list of chaplain posts.[51] Typically a chaplain received four daily rations, fuel, living allowances, plus his monthly salary.

Reverend Michell remained at this post until March 1861, just four months short of five years, making his stay one of the longest terms for any one soldier stationed at Fort Chadbourne.

The early months of 1857 were mainly spent on scouting expeditions for Indians. Overall this year had been relatively quiet.

There was a new Commander at the Department of Texas, Brevet Major General David E. Twiggs, who assumed command on May 18, 1857.

In May, 1st Lt. T. A. Washington, 1st U. S. Infantry, Assistant Quartermaster at Fort Chadbourne, submitted a report to Major D. H. Vinon, Principal Quartermaster, Department of Texas, in compliance with Vinon's earlier request as to establishment, building conditions, water, fuel, forage, hay, beef, roads, transportation, and supplies at Fort Chadbourne. In compliance Washington submitted the following report.

There are nine buildings at the post. Two sets of company quarters, one hundred feet by twenty feet, built of yellow sandstone, and one hospital with the same dimensions and same material, as the company quarters. One storehouse, one hundred feet by twenty feet, used for the Quartermaster and Subsistence Storerooms built of post oak, three post oak frame buildings, officer's quarters, two rooms each, and each with temporary kitchens. Two officer's quarters built of sandstone, one with two rooms, and one of four rooms, and no outhouses. The latter quarters had recently been erected. There was also another stone building in progress of construction, designed for the commanding officer. The work had all been done by enlisted men of the 8th and 1st U. S. Infantry, and the post was now occupied by two Companies of the 1st U. S. Infantry.

The only building material which the country in this vicinity afforded was stone. Fine quarries of soft, homogeneous, sandstone were opened within a few hundred yards of the post, and good stone could be had even nearer. Limestone of a fine quality was four miles distant. On hand were about fifteen thousand feet of assorted pine lumber, hauled from the neighborhood of Bastrop, Texas, and delivered to the fort by contract, at one hundred ten dollars per thousand. About twenty thousand shingles were delivered in the same manner for ten dollars per thousand. Lumber could be hauled by post teams from Fredericksburg or Bastrop, Texas, with a saving to the Government to be ascertained by experiment.

The post water was supplied from Oak Creek about three hundred yards distant, which was a small tributary of the Colorado River. The water was generally good, although the summer before in 1856, like most streams in Texas, it ceased to run. What water there was became unfit for drinking purposes. A small spring was walled in about one and one half miles from the fort, which afforded a sufficient supply of water for drinking and cooking.

Post oak and live oak were abundant for fuel and was of excellent quality. They grew freely on two tracts of land. One was rented from Samuel A. Maverick at twenty-five dollars per month. It contained three hundred twenty acres. The other tract was rented from Howard and Twohig, at fifty dollars per month. The quantity from Howard and Twohig was not specified in the lease. The post proper was on Maverick's land. Fuel was cut and hauled by the command, and was readily procured.

Forage on hand was about two hundred fifty bushels of good quality, and was delivered by contract at two dollars eighty four cents per hundred bushels.

The contract required four thousand bushels from the contractor, I. C. Gooch, and expired on September 30, 1857.

Hay was sparse, but could be had of a good quality from the vicinity of the post. The cost of the hay delivered in 1856, was twenty-five dollars per ton, and was delivered by contract. It was cut in a valley some two miles distant. The grass at this time of the season was sparse, affording scarcely more than enough for good grazing.

Beef was supplied four days per week by contract at nine and half cents per pound, and was of excellent quality. The beef contractor at the time of report was Louis Martin.

There were four roads leading from Fort Chadbourne to other posts. The first road was northeast to Camp Cooper, at a distance of about one hundred five miles, and was in good condition. Streams and water holes were six miles from the post. First was Fish Creek, at nine miles Valley Creek, at sixteen miles Bluff Creek, at twenty-eight miles Comanche Springs, at forty-one miles waterholes, and at sixty-five miles the old fort, Phantom Hill. The streams were easily crossed during all seasons, and the grass was always ample along the route.

The second road was to Fort Mason at a distance of one hundred ten miles. The road lay along Oak Creek for about ten miles, and at twenty-two miles from the post was the Colorado River with brackish water. Twenty-six miles from the post were good watering holes and salt. At thirty-seven miles was the Concho River, with good water, followed by Brady's Creek, then the San Saba River.

The third road was to Fort McKavett at a distance of about ninety-five miles. This was the same road to Fort Mason as far as the Concho. At forty-five miles was Kickapoo Creek, and from that point one traveled along the stream twenty-two miles to its head spring. At twenty-five miles farther was Fort McKavett. The road to the head of the Kickapoo was good, but to McKavett it was very bad. It was rocky and hilly, but there was good grass along the way.

The fourth road was to Camp Colorado, which lay sixty-eight miles from the post. At eight miles were Fish and Valley Creeks on McKay's ranch. At eighteen miles was Bluff Creek. Forty-three miles found watering holes near Round Mountain, and then you reached Camp Colorado. The road was new and not well defined, but generally good with some rocky places. None of the streams enumerated were bridged. The Concho and Colorado Rivers were the only ones which could not be crossed at high water.

As for transportation, stores were hauled either by contract trains (oxen trains) or by public wagons. The cost was two dollars and seventy-five cents per pound.

Supplies were mainly delivered from the Depot in San Antonio, Texas by contract or public wagons. They consisted of subsistence stores and property such as Quartermasters property, clothing, camp and garrison equipage, and the requisite hospital supplies and ordnance stores.

1st Lt. Thornton A. Washington assumed command of Fort Chadbourne for a few short months while Captain John H. King, Company I, 1st U. S. Infantry, left to purchase lumber at the Guadalupe River. There was also a private in Company F, 1st U. S. Infantry assigned to daily duty as the company gardener.

Whether due to Mansfield's visit, or Miller's report of the poor conditions the troops endured at

Fort Chadbourne, there was an increase in building activity during the summer of 1857.

On August 17th, a letter from Captain John Withers, Assistant Adjutant General, Headquarters, Department of Texas, to Captain John H. King, Commander of Fort Chadbourne, informed King that he had made application for three thousand dollars to be expended in the erection and repair of the public buildings at Fort Chadbourne. Captain King was to submit an estimated amount that he deemed necessary to place the officers, men, animals, and government property at Fort Chadbourne under proper shelter. The same letter was sent to Forts Belknap, Cooper, McKavett, Mason, Verde, Davis, Lancaster, Clark, Inge, and Hudson.

Major General Twiggs, in a letter to Colonel Thomas, Assistant Adjutant General of the United States Army, reminded the General that one regiment of the 1st U. S. Infantry in Texas had been living in sheds or tents without wooden floors, for more than ten years. Twiggs respectfully wanted a decision as soon as possible to provide these provisions for the frontier troops.[52]

Many of the enlisted men from Company F, 1ˢᵗ U. S. Infantry, were hired for extra duty activities associated with the construction. Sergeant Bradley was in charge of all extra duty men. There were three masons, three carpenters, one blacksmith, a herder, and five teamsters.

As General Twiggs, Commanding Headquarters, Department of Texas, delved into the task at hand, his observations of the posts situations on the frontier led him to suggest that Forts Brown, McIntosh, and Ringgold Barracks on the Rio Grande, be abandoned. Due to so few troops, and over one thousand four hundred and fifty miles of frontier to guard, he felt the need to apply more pressure in the vicinities where Indian activity required a larger presence of troops. He reasoned, there being no Indians in the areas of the above named posts, that repositioning the troops to the western frontier was a sensible answer to the present situation. Apparently the War Department did not view his suggestion favorably because work continued on the garrisons in the form of new buildings and repair of older ones.

Finally, in 1859, during the Butterfield Overland Mail days, the continual harassment from Indians gave Twiggs another reason to move towards his earlier goal to close several Forts in Texas. Fort Belknap, Fort Brown, Ringgold Barracks, Fort McIntosh, Fort Mason, and Fort McKavett were all on his list.

The long tedious days were sometimes relieved with nothing more than a wagon on the horizon approaching the post. Several wagons probably brought as much excitement as if a party was being planned.

In September a wagon train passed through the post. Appropriations of two hundred thousand dollars were made in 1857 for a partial rerouting and improvement of a road from the Rio Grande to Fort Yuma, on the California side of the Colorado River. James B. Leach with the Department of Interior was Superintendent of the project. The wagon train which left Mississippi on July 1st reached Fort Chadbourne on the 12th of September.

Colonel Leach's health had deteriorated along the trail, so much so that after reaching Fort Chadbourne he remained here along with one ambulance and team that belonged with his wagon train. Assistant Superintendent W. P. Cook took the reigns of the detachment leaving Colonel Leach to recuperate at the fort.[53]

An officer and six men were sent to San Antonio to pick up horses intended for mounting a portion of the Infantry at Fort Chadbourne. Horses and mules were a very important part of military life. Soldiers were expected to care for these animals, and if a horse or mule for that matter was injured, or required to be put down due to ill health, a Board of Survey was assembled. Then it was determined if action would be taken towards the man involved. At Fort Chadbourne in June of 1857, just such a Board was established to investigate Private William Gehring, Company F, 1st U. S. Infantry. A mule in his care was condemned as incurably injured through his neglect, and the board found him guilty. Under paragraph 921, General Regulations of the Army, he would be charged the price of the mule, or if by preference, he could avail himself of the alternative pointed out in that paragraph of the regulations.[54]

Just a few months later another Board of Survey was put together consisting of 1st Lt. S. H. Reynolds, 2nd Lt. C. W. Thomas, and 2nd Lt. J. H. Holman all of the 1st U. S. Infantry. The board met pursuant at 9:00

a.m. on December 29, 1857, to examine and report, upon a sick public horse for which Major Earl Van Dorn, 2nd U. S. Cavalry, was responsible. The board found that the horse in question had very large ulcerative sores upon his back and shoulders, and it was the opinion of the board that it was incurable and recommended the horse be shot.

It was also the Board's opinion that Major Earl Van Dorn should not be held responsible, and that blame should not be attached to any one person in the Military Service. Case was closed.[55]

Chapter VIII

1st Lt. E.E. Phillips

Building Descriptions

Assistant Quartermaster, 2nd Lt. C. W. Thomas, 1st U. S. Infantry did a survey on the Quartermaster's Store at Fort Chadbourne in January 1858. The following items were listed as either worn out. or unfit for use:

7 wagons	2 adzes
6 bridles – ridging	6 augurs assorted
18 bridles – pack	5 bitts augur
2 saddles – pack	6 do brace
4 saddles – wagon	3 chisels
10 single trees	7 chisels framing
1 double tree	3 compasses
2 whips wagon	14 files flat bastard
2 syringes	10 files ½ round
1 buttress	17 files whipsaw

3 files blacksmiths

1 nipper

1 nipper cutting

1 rasp

2 rasp shoeing

1 sledge

1 knife hand, large

1 knife hand, small

1 plane double & smooth

25 axes handles filling

6 brushes whitewash

6 saws assorted

1 saw rip

2 screwdrivers

2 lanterns guarded

2 spoke shaves

2 squares steel

12 trowels

3 trowels pointing

27 axes felling

9 gimlets

1 gimlet spike

3 gauges

9 hatchets

5 hatchets

8 knives drawing

4 axes pick

3 planes fore

6 planes jack

3 wood rasps

6 buckets water

1 diamond glazier

4 forks, hay

6 forks, stable

2 saw sets

1650 sacks grain

29 shovels

1 scale platform

1 sythe

20 spades

In the year of 1858 Fort Chadbourne seemed to go through a quieter period with less correspondence and reports. Of course, the battle for the frontier and Indian Depredations continued, along with the formation of the Texas Mounted Volunteers. But overall, the day to day quantity of information was less than previous years.

One note worthy incident did take place that year. Captain William R. Bradfute, Company G, shot and killed a Private in camp on the Clear Fork of the Brazos. Bradfute was returning from leave. The Captain gave Private William Murray, of Company K an order, and the young Private took exception to Bradfute's tone of voice. The Private then struck the Captain with a violent blow to the face with a clenched fist.

Bradfute staggered from the blow and reacted impulsively by shooting the soldier with his Navy Colt. Captain Bradfute immediately turned himself into the Regimental Commander at Fort Belknap. After a court of inquiry was held at Regimental Headquarters, Captain Bradfute was exonerated and returned to duty at Fort Chadbourne on August 6, 1858, assuming command of the Post.

Several months later the citizens near Fort Belknap instigated proceedings against Captain Bradfute for the shooting of Private Murray. Bradfute was relieved of command at Fort Chadbourne by 2nd

Lt. Aurelius F. Cone, 1st U. S. Infantry, and returned to Fort Belknap. He was released on bail but was never brought to trial against his own wishes to be tried.[56]

A new Assistant Surgeon was also assigned to Fort Chadbourne this year. William H. Babcock arrived in December. He immediately took an assessment of items on hand that belonged to the Medical and Hospital Department of the Army at Fort Chadbourne.

His inventory of supplies on hand included one each of the following medical instruments; amputating, ball forceps, dissecting, obstetrical, pocket, pulley, stomach pump, teeth extractor, trephine, along with six metallic boogies, four silver catheters, and three hernia trusses.

The hospital bedding included thirteen iron bedsteads, twenty-eight bed sacks, sixty blankets, thirty coverlets, eleven gutta-percha clothes, six mattresses, twenty-five mosquito bars, fifty-eight pillow cases, but no pillows are listed, twenty-eight pillow ticks, and ninety-seven sheets.

Hospital stores included three bottles of brandy, thirty-three containers of tea, four bottles of wine and sherry, and four bottles of whiskey.

Under miscellaneous Assistant Surgeon Babcock listed one medicine chest, one rain gauge, two thermometers, and forty towels.[57]

A year later when Assistant Surgeon Charles Smith took the end of year inventory, very little had changed as to hospital supplies. The only count that had increased was the hospital stores. Now listed were twelve bottles of brandy, seventeen bottles of wine, and thirty-six bottles of whiskey.

The New Year at Fort Chadbourne found Captain George W. Wallace in command. One of his first letters of correspondence spoke of a married soldier, Private Toole, whose wife served as a laundress. The young soldier had been assigned to Company G at Fort Chadbourne under Captain Wallace, and he had arrived with his wife. Wallace requested that Private Toole be transferred so that his wife could remain with him. Wallace noted that he could not furnish a ration to the woman in question due to the fact the post already had the authorized number of laundresses. With respect to Mrs. Toole, Captain Wallace noted that she was a decent, proper person, and her husband a sober, steady man, but he was not much of a soldier. Captain Wallace wanted action to be taken sooner than later in order to remedy the situation.

The laundress was one of the few actual jobs a woman could hold at a frontier fort. The position was usually filled by one of the enlisted men's wives, and there were normally two to four laundresses assigned per company. They were paid out of the soldiers pay anywhere from one to four dollars a month, depending on the rank of the soldier. They also received a daily ration of food. They did not associate with the officers wives, who held a certain social standing on the posts, but the laundresses did occasionally serve in other respects, such as a maid, or midwife.

Although these women did serve a purpose, Captain Wallace grew weary of trying to accommodate the ongoing problem of women on the frontier. In 1860, he spoke of a Private in his Company, Alexander Hoyt who was a good soldier, and he had granted him a furlough for re-enlisting. During his absence Hoyt married without the consent of Wallace. Since all the laundress positions were filled at Fort Chadbourne, he needed Hoyt transferred from his company. Wallace wrote, "So many women in a company renders it inefficient; on the march they fill up the wagons with their traps, or wish to do so, and occupy too much of their husbands time in endeavoring to render them comfortable. Once rid of the present batch, hope never again to have more than two laundresses in my company."[58]

Captain Wallace was also in need of a price list for the Rifle Musket, all its parts and accoutrements. The men of his company had broken and lost many articles, and he needed to be able to charge them for the items. He had previously asked for this list from the Chief of Ordnance in San Antonio, but to his irritation he still had received no reply.

Mid year 1st Lt. E. D. Phillips, Assistant Quartermaster, was required under paragraph 982 of the Army Regulations to submit a report on the condition and capacity of the buildings located at Fort Chadbourne. Any additions, alterations, or repairs prior to his arrival in February 1858 were not in his possession, so his report reflected only his knowledge for that time period.

It seemed apparent that year after year, someone would comply with regulations, and comprise and submit the report on building conditions. Seldom though, were there many changes over the years in these reports. If anything, conditions grew steadily worse, and what actual buildings were erected in the first few years continued to deteriorate.

On Lt. Phillip's report there were fourteen usable buildings that could be used as public quarters. Of those, five sets were occupied by officers, a chaplain, and sutler. Besides the public buildings, there were several private buildings which included an ordnance building, sutlers store, and billiard room. (See Fig. 4)

Lt. Phillips made the following suggestions for alterations to tear down the company and hospital kitchens, in order to build new ones. Also, three older buildings that once served as the laundress' quarters should be torn down, and in their place build one good one. The quartermaster and commissary stores, which were now built of picket posts, needed to be rebuilt out of stone.

Repairs suggested were only what Lt. Phillips deemed were absolutely necessary to make these buildings habitable. A new roof and flooring at the hospital, along with constructing new shelves and a counter so it could be used for an up to date dispensary. New roofing was needed on the men's barracks, along with flooring in the ordnance storeroom and Quartermaster's office. There was also a great need for new windows in most of the buildings.

An estimate of materials for additions and alterations accompanied the report. In order to make the troops at this post somewhat comfortable the following materials were needed:

Additions:

Magazine, Stone, 12x14 feet

3000 shingles	200 sheathing boards

15 pine rafters, joist, wall plates

225 feet of plank

14 feet flooring	15 lbs 8 penny nails
25 lbs 5 penny nails	5 lbs 6 penny nails

Kitchen at Officer's Quarters,
Stone, 16x30 feet

7000 Shingles	300 feet pine boards
500 feet sheathing	4 sets window sash
20 pine rafters	1 box window glass
6 pine wall plates	4 kegs 4 penny nails
15 pine rafters	2 kegs 8 penny nails
6 pine wall plates	1 keg 10 penny nails
700 feet plank for flooring	

BUILDING FUNCTION	CONSTRUCTION TYPE	MEASUREMENTS
Quarters (commanding officer)	Adobe with wing and post oak picket kitchen, porch under construction; building decaying, adobe walls exposed to rain, otherwise tolerable condition.	19 ft x 38 ft (main room) 19 ft x 10 ft (wing) 17 1/3 ft x 42 ½ ft (kitchen)
Quarters (chaplain, lieutenant)	Oak, 3 rooms and post oak picket kitchen; beginning to decay	Overall 15 ft x 37 ft (3 rooms of 20, 18, and 13 ft) 14 ½ ft x 30 ft (kitchen)
Quarters (doctor, lieutenant)	Brown sandstone, 4 room with 10 foot passageway, brown sandstone kitchen; very good condition	Overall 33 ft x 52 ft 2 rooms 18 ½ ft x 21 ft 2 bedrooms 14 1/3 ft x 21 ft 10 ft passageway
Quarters (post sutler)	Post oak pickets, 2 room with passageway and post oak kitchen; among first buildings constructed at post, timber somewhat rotten, but quarters inhabitable.	17 ft 14 in x 41 ft 3 in overall 2 rooms 13 ft x 19 ft 9 ft 3 in passageway 14 ½ ft x 27 ft kitchen
Adjutant's Office	Sandstone, 2 room, 4-5 years old; not fit to be occupied, decayed and defective roof, walls good	19 ½ ft x 19 ½ ft, one room 19 ½ ft x 13 1/3 ft, one room
Men's Quarters	Brown sandstone, dirt floors with picket kitchen; quarters in passable condition, roofs need considerable repairs, kitchen a miserable concern and not fit to be used.	22 ft x 101 ft each (quarters) 17 ft x 33 ft (kitchen)
Laundress's Quarters (old; once occupied by officers)	Oak timber, 2 room; dilapidated but reparable	16 ft x 41 overall 19 ft and 22 ft rooms
Laundress's Quarters (new) built after April 1859	Post oak pickets, 1 room, no floors or kitchens	15 ft x 30 ft
Laundress's Quarters (new) built after April 1859	Post oak pikets, 1 room, no floors or kitchens	15 ft x 30 ft
(not designated)	Oak, several years old; no floors, old canvas roofs, nearly worthless and nearly uninhabitable	15 ½ ft x 15 ½ ft
(not designated)	Oak, several years old; no floors, old canvas roofs, nearly worthless and nearly uninhabitable	12 ft x 20 ¼ ft
(not designated)	Oak, several years old; no floors, old canvas roofs, nearly worthless and nearly uninhabitable	14 ft x 17 ½ ft
Hospital	Sandstone, 3 room (ward room, dispensary, and storeroom); no floors, shelving, etc.	24 ft x 65 ft overall 26 ft (ward room) 20 ft (dispensary) 15 ft (storeroom)
Hospital Kitchen	Oak pickets, comparatively new; decayed and old	15 ft x 16 ft
Quartermaster's office and ordnance storeroom	Oak pickets, 2 room; no floor	17 ft each room
Subsistence storehouse	Post oak timber; old, hardly fit for purpose	20 ft x 101 ft
Guardhouse	Oak, 2 room; tolerable condition	15 ½ ft x 27 ½ ft overall 17 ft (guard room) 10 ½ ft (prisoners' room)
Baker house with oven	Oak timber; too small	12 ft x 18 ft 12 1.2 ft (oven)
Blacksmith's shop	Very poor old building, almost falling from decay and age	16 ft x 18 ft
Lime House	Pickets and covered with old canvas; one of oldest structures	17 ft x 17 ½ ft
Quartermaster's yard, stables, forage house, etc.	Enclosure formed by heavy oaken pickets, 2 sides occupied by stables (1 shingled, 1 not)	285 ft x 269 ft Stable 13 ft wide 13 ½ ft x 66 ft (forage house)
Ordnance sergeant's quarters	Oak, very good condition	18 ft x 39 ft
Sutler's Store	No material indicated	No dimensions provided
Billiard Room	No material indicated	No dimensions provided

Description of Fort Chadbourne, June 30, 1859 (Philliips)

Fig: 4

Alterations:

One Company Kitchen, Stone 20x30 feet

18000 Shingles	40 pine rafters
2000 feet sheathing	400 feet pine boards
12 pine wall plates	6 pine tie beams
20 pieces pin scantling	12 sets window sash
2 boxes window glass	5 kegs 4 penny nails
3 kegs 8 penny nails	2 kegs 10 penny nails
10000 shingles	1500 feet sheathing
28 pine rafters	

Captain George Wallace spent much of the rest of the year recruiting, and was furnished two hundred dollars for this purpose.

He placed an order with the Adjutant General's office in Washington D. C. requesting blank forms be sent to him at Fort Chadbourne, via the St. Louis and California Overland Mail route. He felt the mail would reach him in half the time it would from the San Antonio area. His order was for forty re-enlistment forms, twenty enlistment forms, twenty-four regimental recruiting returns, twelve accounts of current recruiting, twelve certificates for pension, and twelve certificates of disability.

When one thinks of the frontier, a band does not come to mind, but Fort Chadbourne was known to have a very good band. Captain Wallace hoped to re-enlist Thomas Hanlon, who had previously enlisted at the age of fourteen and was a good fifer. At the last minute Hanlon decided not to re-enlist, so Wallace attempted to requisition for a new fifer to fill the vacancy. In the meantime a letter from an unidentified writer at Fort Chadbourne was mailed to a newspaper, The Pilot Office, in Boston, Massachusetts. After reading it, Patrick Donahue, the editor of the newspaper, forwarded it to the Secretary of War, and the Secretary to Adjutant General S. Cooper. A portion of the letter is paraphrased below:

"I am going to unfold a few lines to the ignorant citizens stating how the poor unfortunate soldiers are used in Company G, 1st U. S. Infantry at Fort Chadbourne. First, I will commence about the first sergeant of the Company. He is starving himself and the men to save some Company funds for the Captain of said Company which he uses for gambling money. The first Sergeant is a tyrant. He flogs the men which he has no right to do. If the men go to the Captain they will not get any satisfaction from him for he loves his first sergeant too well as to check up on him about flogging the men. There is a poor unfortunate little drummer in the company which the first sergeant treats like a dog. The sergeant is a black hearted villain. He has the prettiest face man ever laid eyes on, a very pretty short nose, and chow bones. His head is like a Jackasses head, and a very pretty smile he has on his countenance. When he speaks to any of the Privates he is meaner than the buzzard which flies about the prairie picking up every thing that they can get. If the poor soldiers were to get all their rations they would not be starved. The poor soldiers only get but one quarter, and the other three quarters does the officers for gambling money. For breakfast they get some rotten pork and a little coffee. For dinner they get some rice soup and a piece of beef which is of no account. For supper there is some water which they call coffee. Then at the same time the poor soldiers have to work as hard as any laboring man in the states which gets one dollar a day. The soldiers work from seven in the morning until half past twelve. From half past twelve they have rest until two o'clock in the afternoon. Then they go to work from two until a half hour before sundown, and so on, until Sundays.

They have Sundays to rest their weary bones. P. S. One thing I forgot to tell the citizens, the Orderly Sergeants name is John Sheld[59]".

General Cooper recommended sending Captain Withers to investigate the allegations against Captain Wallace and the First Sergeant, but the investigation was carried out by Captain E. K. Smith, 2nd U. S. Cavalry, Camp Colorado.

Captain Smith proceeded to Fort Chadbourne in November 1859, and presented himself to the Commanding Officer, Captain Wallace of Company G, 1st U. S. Infantry. Captain Wallace furnished him with the latest muster roll, and asked that the investigation be carried out without his presence in order to abstain from influencing his men in their statements.

Captain Smith chose non-commissioned officers and privates, and obtained the following statements:

"That the men of Company G, 1st U. S. Infantry receive an abundant supply of rations; that in addition to the regulation allowance the company mess is furnished with vegetables purchased with the company fund by the Captain and that the men of the Company are contented and satisfied, and that they have no complaints to make either against the Captain or 1st Sergeant; that the 1st Sergeant is not tyrannical in the exercise of his authority and that the men are not flogged; that the Captain of the Company G, 1st U. S. Infantry listens to the complaints made to him by the men of his company, and that they have no cause to be dissatisfied with the justice of his decisions.

"Examining the Company Council book, I found the accounts correct and properly audited, and that there was no misappropriation of the fund as set forth in the letter to the Adjutant Generals Office.

"I find as the result of the investigation that the letter above referred to was probably written by a drummer boy discharged in October last, which boy, from the statement made by the men under examination was a wild bad boy who took this mode of renting his spite upon the 1st Sergeant for having been punished by him, and that the letter is a base slander of an officer, proverbial through the Department and with his brother officers for his care and attention to his men and for the interest he takes in the welfare of his company.

"On the muster roll for Company G, 1st U. S. Infantry for September and October 1859 handed me by its Company Commander, I noticed the names of ten men who had then reenlisted in the company; this fact is the strongest evidence of the absence of abuse and injustice in the administration of the affairs of the company."

Captain Wallace was unsatisfied with the War Department, and continued to convey his displeasure at their handling of the whole affair. He was later reprimanded for his ongoing rampage. Although he and his 1st Sergeant were exonerated of any wrong doing, in January 1860, Wallace was still agitated and continued to look for the writer responsible for the letter. In his letter to Captain Daniel Huston, Company D, 1st U. S. Infantry, he had decided that the young fifer, who was discharged in November, was the culprit. Wallace originally felt the young man was good but now ascertained doubt, and was convinced that the boy was a great scoundrel in the vilest manner.

After much deliberation, the editor Patrick Donahue, sent the original document to Adjutant General Cooper, and the writer was identified as F. H. Good, Company G, 1st U. S. Infantry.

In February, Captain Wallace penned another letter to Captain Huston concerning his poor judgment in the musician Hanlon, and regretted his assuming the worse of the young man. He explained he had since learned that Hanlon had nothing to do with the letter to the Boston newspaper, but in fact, it was a discharged drummer boy from his company that had caused all the trouble. Wallace felt remorse for his injustice of Hanlon, and wished to withdraw the charge.[60]

The rest of the year saw several new recruits. June brought Lt. Colonel Gouverneur Morris, who assumed Command of the post upon his arrival, along with the non commissioned staff and band of the 1st U. S. Infantry. Recruits from Company I joined in July, plus six recruits from Company G, and eleven from Company H in December. Texas Ranger, James Buckner Barry made a stop at the post while scouting for Indians on the Clear Fork. A report that Indians had killed several teamsters along the Butterfield Route led the Ranger's on inspections of the area.

In November, a General Court Martial concerning Ordnance Sergeant Dudley Johnson, a soldier serving at the post since 1854, was held at Fort Chadbourne. An altercation between Quartermaster Sergeant John Sheld, 1st U. S. Infantry, also acting as

Commissary Sergeant, and Sergeant Johnson, took place concerning Sergeant Johnson's allocation of fresh beef. Sheld believed Johnson was only due two pounds of beef, while Johnson thought he had another six or seven pounds allocated to him. When Johnson questioned Sheld, Sheld took the offensive and began to swear at Sergeant Johnson, and placed Sergeant Johnson under arrest.

Sheld still irate, complained that Sergeant Johnson had not obeyed his orders to stay in his quarters under arrest, and had ventured out to the garden. Johnson's defense was that he did not feel Sergeant Sheld had the power to arrest him since they were both of the same rank.

Even so, Johnson was brought up on the charge of conduct to the prejudice of good order and military discipline. His charges read:

"1st: In this that Ordnance Sergeant Dudley Johnson, U. S. Army, did use highly abusive and insubordinate language towards John Sheld, Quartermaster Sergeant and acting Commissary Sergeant of the Post.

"2nd: That Ordnance Sergeant Dudley Johnson, U. S. Army, on being ordered in arrest by John Sheld,

Quartermaster Sergeant did say "You put me in arrest, you damn puke, you have no right to do so."

"3rd: In this that Ordnance Sergeant Dudley Johnson, U. S. Army, being in arrest did leave his quarters and go about the Post of Fort Chadbourne without permission from proper authority. "

Although Sgt. Johnson had several soldiers testify in his defense, he was still found guilty on all three counts. He was sentenced to forfeit sixteen dollars of his pay per month for twelve months, and to be suspended from his rank as Ordnance Sergeant for the same period.

In 2002, Carol Carpenter, the great great granddaughter of Dudley Johnson filed an application for correction of military record. The family believed the record to be in error, or unjust, due to the following: the prosecution witnesses supported Sergeant Johnson and not the charge held against him; that Quartermaster Sheld had no authority to place Sergeant Johnson under arrest due to the two holding the same rank; and the legal order for his arrest was not issued until after Sergeant Johnson was accused of disobeying the order of leaving his quarters.

On June 16, 2004, the family received a letter from the Army Board for Correction of Military Records. It stated that action by the Board, in relationship to court-martials, may extend only to correction of a sentence for the purposes of clemency, but cannot disturb the finality of a general court-martial conviction. That means that while the Board could change Johnson's sentence, it did not have the authority to overturn or nullify the court-martial conviction.

As of late, Ms. Carpenter was continuing her quest to defend her great great grandfather, and was proceeding through other channels to clear his name of any misdeed.[61]

Chapter IX

Surrender of

Fort Chadbourne

There have been so many accounts of the Civil War, that I have chosen to forgo in detail that part which has been covered in numerous memoirs and history books throughout the years, but rather stay close to home and touch on the details that surround Fort Chadbourne and its contributions to that era.

In late 1860 the approach of the Civil War cast a dark shadow. The Governor of Texas, Sam Houston, was called upon by the people of this state to arrange a special session of the legislature in order to discuss the approaching need for secession. Governor Houston's refusal to convene this special session caused the people to petition him. Even after petitions from all over the state were received, the Governor was neglected to abide by the peoples wishes.

This led to a call for a convention which would essentially bypass the government. A call for the election of delegates was made and circulated by the end of 1860, with the actual meeting scheduled for January 28, 1861 in Austin. At the convention the Texas Ordinance of Secession was adopted that separated Texas from the United States by a vote of one hundred sixty-six to eight.

The convention empowered a committee composed of twenty-one members with John C. Robertson[62] acting as chairman, to free Texas of the federal troops now occupying the state in the numerous posts scattered along the frontier.

The appointed commissioners were to confer with General David Twiggs, then Commander of the Department of Texas in San Antonio, to accomplish the surrender at the Department of Texas Headquarters. The main objective was to secure the property and all munitions of war belonging to the United States Government. Among these appointed commissioners was Samuel A. Maverick, who owned the property that several federal forts were now located on in the State of Texas, including Fort Chadbourne.

Other committee members were P. N. Luckett, and Thomas J. Devine.

When General Twiggs did not hastily comply with these commissioners, Colonel Ben McCulloch[63] chosen to lead the Texas forces was urged to procure a sufficient number of troops to overpower the federal forces located in San Antonio. The assembled Texas Volunteers under dark of night entered San Antonio, occupied positions around the quarters of the federal troops, and demanded the surrender of General Twiggs, along with all public property. General Twiggs quickly surrendered and the United States troops were told to evacuate Texas. Unionist would be permitted to retain their side arms and garrison equipage if they quickly departed Texas soil. General Twiggs surrendered all federal military posts in Texas. Colonel Ben McCulloch had the responsibility of immediately securing these posts.[64]

The next day General Twiggs, who was now being accused of treason to his country for submitting to the Texas troops, was relieved of his command. He was replaced by Colonel Carlos A. Waite who had been stationed at Fort Chadbourne since June 1860. Twiggs, who was in his seventies, was later given a position in the Confederate States Army, but in 1862, he died of pneumonia.

The Texas frontier was divided into three districts. John S. Ford commanded from the Rio Grande to Brownsville, Ben McCulloch assumed command from Fort Chadbourne to the Rio Grande, and his brother Henry McCulloch, from Fort Chadbourne to the Red River.

The time had now come for the military establishments in Texas to surrender themselves and their munitions to the Texas Regimental Forces. The United States Stars and Stripes would be lowered, the Stars and Bars flag raised, and Texas would now stand proud in its southern heritage beside its confederate brothers.

Noah Smithwick once noted in his diary that riding into Fort Chadbourne, and seeing the absence of the American flag flying where it had fanned the breeze for so long, was the first visible sign of the impending war.[65]

Colonel Henry McCulloch ordered Captains Thomas Frost, Robert Bonner Halley, Thomas Harrison, James Buckner Barry, H. A. Hamner, and D. C. Cowan, who had previously been authorized to raise companies of Texas Mounted Rangers for use in the protection of the frontier against Indians. Calling on his Rangers, many refused to join this assault against the federal forces. This caused difficulty in raising a sufficient force, but with the Rangers who were willing, along with other Texas volunteers, he was able to assemble approximately two hundred men, and organized them into Companies under Captains Frost, Robert Halley, and Barry.

On February 28, 1861, Lt. Colonel Gouverneur Morris, 1st U. S. Infantry, Commanding Fort Chadbourne, reported to Colonel Waite, now in command of the Department of Texas concerning the surrender of Fort Chadbourne. He contended in compliance with General Orders No. 5, that he had entered into a written agreement with Colonel Henry McCulloch, to deliver the public property at Fort Chadbourne. This included two twelve-pound brass mountain howitzers,[66] and ordnance stores, numerous veterinary, blacksmith, and hand tools, camp and garrison equipage, along with furniture and medicines which were turned over to Lieutenant A. K. Leigh acting as assistant quartermaster for the Texas Army.

Colonel Morris agreed to depart the premises as soon as transportation could be sent there to move his command. Colonel Morris needed approximately thirteen wagons to move himself, one captain, one assistant surgeon, one second lieutenant, one chaplain, and servants, which consisted of one man, four women, and three children of Company G, 1st U. S. Infantry. Also laundresses and children belonging to Company G, together with a detachment of Company I troops, their laundresses, a hospital matron, stores, and post records.

In reply to all posts concerning surrender, Colonel Waite under Special Order No. 41, ordered that all troops including the troops at Fort Chadbourne to march for the coast and await further transportation upon their arrival at Green Lake some twenty miles from Indianola. On March 2nd thirteen wagons and teams left San Antonio to transport troops located at Forts Chadbourne and Mason to the coast.

Finally on March 23, 1861, Company G abandoned Fort Chadbourne, leaving Captain R. B. Halley of the Texas Mounted Riflemen in command. They arrived on April 15, 1861, at Green Lake, Texas. Major Caleb C. Sibley assumed command at Green

Lake, and marched the entire command, which included Company G, 1st U. S. Infantry from Fort Chadbourne, to Indianola for boarding on the "Star of the West". Sibley loaded all troops and camp equipment on two small steamers and proceeded out into the bay in search of that ship. He found that both the "Star of the West", and the gunboat "Mohawk", which had been assigned to guard it, were gone. On April 23rd, Sibley chartered two schooners, the "Horace" and the "Urbana". The troops were loaded on the two boats, and were towed down the bay by the "Fashion", but the weather became violent. A gale prevented the schooners from crossing for the next few days.

At daylight on the morning of April 25, 1861, Major Sibley awoke and found General Nichols, assistant to Colonel Earl Van Dorn, with three ships forebodingly just across the bar from his two schooners. Colonel Van Dorn dispatched a message to Sibley requesting a meeting to arrange for the peaceful surrender of the Federal forces. Sibley quickly agreed to Van Dorn's demand that his entire force be placed as prisoners of war, but Van Dorn agreed to parole them immediately to any and all who would take an oath not to bear arms, or exercise any function against the Confederacy, until properly exchanged. This included Company G, 1st U. S. Infantry, from Fort Chadbourne, the post he had commanded in 1858.

The following articles of agreement were entered into between Major C. C. Sibley, of the United States Army, and Colonel Earl Van Dorn, of the Confederate States Army: "It is stipulated and agreed to that the United States troops, officers and men, shall become prisoners of war, with the privilege of giving their paroles of honor, if officers, and their oaths, if soldiers, not to bear arms or exercise any of the functions of their office, under their commissions or enlistments, against the Confederate States of America, unless an exchange of prisoners shall be made or until released by the authority of the President of the Confederate States; the arms and equipments of the men and all the public property in the possession of the company commanders to be given up to an agent appointed for the purpose, on board the transport which shall be employed to convey those who may desire it to the United States, private property to be unmolested. Above stated shall be allowed to pass unmolested through the Confederate States of America, by the way of Galveston and up the Mississippi River, any point they may see fit to go within the limit of the United States of America, or by any other route they may see fit to take".

Oaths and parole papers were completed, and Sibley's command was divided into three groups. Company G, from Fort Chadbourne was loaded on the "Horace" and preceded to New York, arriving on May 31, 1861, which took an entire month from the coast of Texas.[67]

Chapter X

Sidney Green Davidson

Sidney Green Davidson had a loving family, but along with his southern upbringing he had another family to also serve; his Texas and Confederate brothers. On May 9, 1862, countless soldiers passed the long hours of boredom by writing to loved ones, and so much of what they related during that time was of course the realization of what lay ahead for the country. Davidson was one of those men who loyally wrote to his dear wife Mary every chance he got, and she in turn answered those letters with love from home. His letters were always signed in the exact same way, "Yours ever, S. G. Davidson", and hers in return were signed, "Yours in love, Mary." You will note his final letter home is my reason for bringing your attention to their closings.

History can be passed down through nothing more than hearsay, taken from correspondence, diaries, or memoirs of those involved. Occasionally we become lucky, and families have saved and treasured personal mementos and letters from one generation to the other, such as, the letters between Sidney Green Davidson, and Mary Kuykendall Davidson. These letters allow us to travel back in time and share with them the thoughts of those who penned them.

Sidney Green Davidson was born in Tennessee and came to Texas in the 1850's. He married Mary Kuykendall in 1856, and they had three children. In February 1861, Colonel Henry McCulloch asked for volunteers to form the 1st Texas Mounted Rifles. Sidney Green Davidson never hesitated and joined immediately as part of Captain R. B. Halley's Company. Soon afterward Davidson was elected 1st Lieutenant.

Davidson's letters began in January 1861, and found him in route from Austin, Texas, via Brownwood, Camp Colorado, and finally arriving at his destination Fort Chadbourne. These accounts were full of his ideas, his worries, his hopes, along with the love he had for his family. In January he explained to his dear wife Mary that before the letter he was writing reached her, Texas would be a free and independent republic. In February he, along with his company, was in Brownwood, on the way to Camp Colorado. It had uneventfully fallen into their hands by unconditional surrender of all property. Captain Thomas Frost was left in command of that post, and Davidson wrote that Camp Cooper had been taken by Captain Dalrymple and his Company. Davidson's company then marched to Fort Chadbourne which was located sixty miles away.

Davidson had to share the post for several weeks with the federal troops, who were still at Fort Chadbourne, awaiting transportation to the coast. When they left, the Texas Mounted Rifles took full possession of the post. Colonel McCulloch had assigned them to Fort Chadbourne, and it would serve as their Headquarters. After the federal troops left, Davidson informed Mary, they now occupied Fort Chadbourne and that he had got "good quarters".

His description of Fort Chadbourne called it a pretty post, but the dullest place in the world. They received no news except from the St. Louis Republican Newspaper. One bright spot he mentioned was the young daughter of Captain Wallace of the regular army. He told Mary the little girl was sweet and a treat that he would miss when she was gone. She made him think of home and his own small children.

He told Mary his separation from her and the kids was not pleasant, but he loved the service, and the wild life he was leading. One can feel the love he had for his dear ones, but at the same time this new adventure lured him away from them. It captured his inner need for being a part of protecting his beliefs, and serving his country in their time of need. He always reminded his wife he would either be home to see her, or find a way for her and the children to come to him. Sadly this would never be.

Mary answered every letter he sent with one of her own telling her dear husband of the comings and goings of friends and family. There had been some fevers in the area, some had died, but she and the kids had remained quite well. Rain had fallen, the corn had come up, and the youngest son George, sat in her lap and talked about his papa. He wanted to be a ranger just like his papa. She also commented on an article in the paper concerning approximately one thousand rangers being raised for frontier service. She asked her husband if he would be discharged once those men were in place.

By April many of McCulloch's men were out on scouting trips. Davidson had received orders authorizing him to raise a company for twelve months service. On May 10, 1861, at Fort Chadbourne, Davidson's Company was mustered into the Confederate States Army and known as the First Regiment, Texas Mounted Rifles. Along with Davidson the following men joined Company F, Privates Asa F. Bellamy, Henry Ludlow, Wiley Hamilton, Samuel Gallatin, Thomas Leath, Duncan McNair, M. Columbus Mackey, G. R. Kuykendall, Nathal J. Franklin, James C. Marshal, B. Oliver Morris, William C. Morris, Columbus Nayler, Edward Pace, Robert M. Scott, Samuel Shelton, George W. Warren, 2nd Lt. James S. Bigham, Surgeon Jesse A. Dereson, and Sergeants Edward Rancier and Jeremiah D. Scott.

When Davidson wrote and informed his wife of this information he added some unpleasant news. He told her it would be at least another month before he could get home to see her and the children. He was considering bringing her and the children, to Fort Chadbourne to live with him, if he remained at the post. He wanted to find a good family to stay at their family home while they were absent. He requested

119

twenty-five or thirty dollars as he had not been paid by the government since his arrival, and he really needed some money to see him through. He asked Mary to drop a line to some friends telling them he had held a place for them in his company, and for the men to get a move on. He added she should write to him and let Lt. Bigham bring a return letter back with him.

Finally in June, Davidson started for home. While on his way he wrote another letter to Mary from Camp Colorado. He was headed home when an express arrived from Colonel Henry McCulloch. McCulloch would be arriving at Fort Chadbourne in a few days time, and required Davidson to be there. So Davidson had no choice but to cancel his planned trip home. He wrote, "I would have loved to have gone home. It would have afforded me more pleasure than all things, but I must serve my country first".

Camp Colorado was now to be garrisoned by twenty men from Fort Chadbourne who would replace Captain Thomas Frost's Company. Those men departed immediately to the Red River. Within a matter of a few months, Captain Frost would be listed on Fort Chadbourne post returns as Commander of the Post, and continued to serve in that position through early 1862.

June 7, 1861, Davidson wrote that his Company was now complete. He told Mary to tell Bell and Gaston, the friends whose arrival he had been awaiting, that they should remain there as he had no room for them at the time. He said that if he continued to hold them a space while men were standing in line to assume those positions, it would have made him look bad within his company and he could not risk that.

There was plenty to do here, as the Indians were thick! "I am still not sure when I can return home for a visit. It could be twelve months or a few days. Keep your spirits up Mary."

On June 17, 1861, Captain Sidney Green Davidson wrote the last letter Mary would ever receive from him:

"Dear Mary,

Again I am disappointed but not as usual disagreeably. Lt. Col. Frost who is stationed at this post has just arrived here and starts on a scout to the head of Colorado River in the morning. As it will be the last chance for Indians until fall I have determined

121

to go along. We will be gone 20 days and I hope and trust that we may do something in that time. When I return I shall go home. There are now two Companies (100) men stationed at this Post. Capt. John's Company and my Company. The boys are all well and in high spirits. We drill every day, the boys are very fond of it. Mary, I have no more to say now – no instructions to give, for I know that you will do all that you can. I will come home just as soon as I can but I won't neglect my duties to do it. My love to all. Kiss the children for me. God bless you all.

Goodbye

S. G. Davidson"

Earlier your attention was brought to the fact that in every single letter home, Davidson always signed his letters to Mary as, "yours ever". In his last letter to her it was signed, "Goodbye". Whether a premonition, a simple coincidence, or just in a hurry to quickly jot Mary a note before his scouting trip, the letter is foreboding of what was to come.

On June 23, 1861, Sidney Green Davidson met his death never to write to Mary again. A description appeared in the Belton Democrat. To summarize, Sidney Green Davidson on a scouting party with

Colonel Frost, camped approximately five miles below Big Spring at the head of the Colorado. A report came in that there were fires still burning at an Indian camp that had recently been deserted up the road. Frost's command spotted a body of Indians, eight in number, well mounted and in full gallop. Colonel Frost formed the command in a line and gave the signal to attack. Unfortunately some of the men broke free of the main line due to the swiftness of their horses, and Sidney Green Davidson being well mounted was quickly in the lead. After galloping for five or six miles Davidson caught up with the Indians and dashed between two of them firing upon them. They dismounted and shot him in the heart just before he passed them, and the other put two arrows in his back immediately after he passed, which killed him instantly. The men in the rear now opened fire, killing one of the Indians and continuing the charge on the others. Some stopped to see if they could render aid to Captain Davidson. Those who continued the charge saw two of the Indians being held on their horses by others, and one appeared to be fatally wounded.

Since the horses were exhausted the men returned to camp at Big Spring. After reaching camp just before nightfall seventeen Indians appeared on a ridge southwest of the camp and challenged the scouting part to fight. Lt. Colonel Frost with a few of his men rode upon an elevation to the north of camp and saw a large body of Indians east of the camp. Apparently a trap was being set, but Colonel Frost did not take the bait. In the wee hours of the night there was an attempt to steal some of the pack mules, and two Yager rifles were fired into the camp but no one was injured.

Due to the condition of the horses and the scanty supply of ammunition Colonel Frost returned his command to Fort Chadbourne.

The body of Captain Sidney Green Davidson was buried near the Big Spring.[68]

At this point, correspondence slows almost to a standstill concerning Fort Chadbourne. Colonel Henry McCulloch issued an order regarding mail on August 1, 1861. Beginning at Asylum Creek there was no detachment stationed between there and Camp Colorado. Once the mail reached Camp Colorado on Friday, it then arrived at Fort Chadbourne on Sunday, leaving there on Monday and reaching the troops stationed on the Concho on Tuesday.

Returning mail would leave the Concho area on Sunday, reach Chadbourne on Monday, leave there on Tuesday and reach Camp Colorado on Thursday. The command at Chadbourne carried the mail from here to Camp Colorado, and then the troops at the Concho carried it from Chadbourne to their Camp.[69]

Colonel McCulloch wrote his mother about his brother Ben who he had not heard from in over a month. He was anxious to be with him and engage in more active service. After a ten day rest at Camp Colorado he was on his way to Fort Chadbourne for an expedition.

In the fall and early 1862, troops were rallied for expeditions for scouting parties. This included Fort's Belknap, Cooper, Camp Colorado and Fort Chadbourne.

After the twelve month enlistment ran out in April 1862, the men were mustered out of duty at Fort Mason. They had a choice to make; return to frontier duty, or enlist in the Eighth Texas Cavalry Battalion, which became part of the First Texas Cavalry. Most chose to reenlist.

By mid 1862 the paper trail with anything concerning Fort Chadbourne went dry until near

Christmas time 1864. At that time troops once again appeared to be forming Indian expeditions for capturing, and redirecting any Indians found on the frontier. In January 1865, Texas State troops, along with Confederate forces, located Indians camped on a creek in present day Tom Green County. This would soon become the controversial Battle of Dove Creek.

Chapter XI

Dove Creek

Confederate troops assembled at Fort Chadbourne in early January 1865, under the command of Captain Henry Fossett, with the intention of a scouting trip in search of Indians. An earlier such trip by Captain N. M. Gillintine of the Texas Militia had reported signs of a large, but deserted encampment in the area.

At the post, dispatched by James Buckner Barry, in reply to a letter dated December 9, 1864, Fossett was joined by Lt. J. A. Brooks, Lt. J. R. Giddens, and Lt. J. R. Carpenter with sixty men, Jack Cureton with seventeen men from the First Frontier District, and Lt. Martin of Brown County with thirty men for a total of one hundred sixty one men. These men were composed of Companies A & B stationed at Camp Colorado, Companies G & H stationed at Camp McCord, and Company D stationed at Fort Belknap.

127

The men were ordered to turn over the command to the senior officer at Fort Chadbourne, and to work in accord with any state troops that were there.

Captain S. S. Totton was in command of approximately 325 state militia men, which included Captains R. S. Barnes and W. A. Cathey of Johnson County, James Cunningham of Comanche County, G. Graham of Coryell County, and N. M. Gillintine and William H. Culver of Erath County. They were dispersed under Special Order No. 31, to aid in the scouting trip.

Totton was well aware they were to ride to Fort Chadbourne to meet up with troops there, but instead Totton decided to follow the trail Captain Gillintine had located earlier, and ignored the orders given him for state and federal troops to work in concurrence.

After waiting for two days at Fort Chadbourne, Commander Fossett became impatient while awaiting the arrival of the state troops. He ordered his forces to set out for the Colorado River in order to locate the Indian trail. The very next day they located two abandoned Indian camps. When they reached the North Concho, Fossett's men counted approximately one hundred and fifty wigwams that had been in the vicinity within the last week.   They remained in this area for two days sending scouts ahead and continuing to wait on Captain Totton's men. On January 7th, the report came that the Indians were camped on Dove Creek. Fossett assumed that Totton had followed another trail, and rather than wait any longer, readied his troops to advance on the camps the next day.   By afternoon, the soldiers were approximately twelve miles from Dove Creek, and by nightfall were ready to march. Before midnight Captains Barnes, Gillintine, and Culver from Totton's militia, rode into the Confederate camp and reported that Totton's state troops were fifteen miles in the rear. After conferring with Fossett, the three Captains carried the information back to Totton who hurriedly moved his troops ahead for a coordinated attack with Fossett's men.

The next day the state militia arrived in the vicinity of Dove Creek. Concealed behind a small hill, Totton and Fossett held a last minute meeting, and quickly drew up a battle plan. Although Fossett outranked Totton, he declined to command.[70]

The plan between Confederate and State troops consisted of a rendezvous point one mile north of the

Indian camp. Both Fossett and Totton, without any attempt to establish communication with the Indians, decided to attack.

The state militia would circle to the left of the hill moving in an easterly direction, dismount, wade across the creek, and attack from the north. Fossett's men would circle the hill to the south and west in order to cut off the herd of Indian horses, then attack the camp from the southwest side of Dove Creek.

Without any regard to a peaceful resolution, the decision was made to attack. The Indians outnumbering the troops approximately two to one had chosen their campsite for its natural defense position. Encamped in a large grove of trees in the forks of Dove Creek, the campsite sat high giving the Indians an advantage.

In the end the battle plan would be hugely criticized. Without following a strategic military plan, both Fossett and Totton led troops into an eventual massacre of their men. Expecting to spring a surprise attack on the Indians it was their military manpower that was quickly attacked by the rifle laden Indians hidden in dense underbrush. The Indians easily picked off the troops as they made their way into camp. The State troops, who had crossed the knee deep creek to attack, were quickly overtaken and had to withdraw.

The Confederates left on their own continued the attack, but would never claim victory. At the end of day four Confederates were killed, and five wounded, along with eighteen state militia killed and nineteen wounded. It would later be reported by the Kickapoo Indians that twelve of their tribe were killed, and eight wounded.[71]

Over a foot of snow had fallen the day following the attack. The men were beaten, wounded, hungry, frigidly freezing to death, and saddened by the loss of their friends. Litters were built from sticks and wet blankets to haul the wounded; the dead buried near Dove Creek. With nothing to eat the men butchered horses to survive.

The Indians packed up their humble belongings, deserted their camp, and although they had wounded and dead, their continued journey to the Mexican border was made with pride for the battle they had fought and survived.

Following this fiasco, for years the usually friendly Kickapoo Indians would seek revenge crossing the border over and over into Texas, destroying property, killing innocent victims, and carrying off women and children. It wasn't until 1873, when Colonel Ranald Mackenzie led an organized raid into Mexico killing, capturing, and setting fire to Indian encampments, that the repercussions of Dove Creek would finally end.

Fossett and Totton made a grave mistake that day. First they did not follow rules of engagement. They never considered a reasonable outcome, only attack and kill. Perhaps the men that died that day would not feel their lives were lost in vain, but as history would show, this massacre could have been prevented. If the Commanders had done their job, and made any attempt whatsoever to make contact with these Indians, these lives may have been spared. Their years on the frontier alone should have told them that this overly large band of Indians, with a permanent campsite in this area, would be a friendly tribe. But these Commanders were never interested in that. They wanted a battle, expecting to brag of a big victory when it was over, and instead they got more than they bargained for. It would cost the frontier settlers of Texas eight long years of hell.

Chapter XII

Reestablish

Fort Chadbourne

Following the Battle of Dove Creek there is little mention of Fort Chadbourne as the Civil War comes to an end. It would be early 1867 before it would once again be considered as a major frontier post, and its paper trail would once again reappear.

Correspondence in February between Bvt. Major General Charles Griffin, Commander, District of Texas, and Bvt. Major General George L. Hartsuff, A.A.G. Department of the Gulf, New Orleans, LA, discussed the need of establishing a permanent military post either at Camp Colorado or at Fort Chadbourne for protection of settlers. Griffin, in accord with an earlier communication with General John Hatch, was also inclined to give preference to Fort Chadbourne.

133

However, he did not think Fort Mason should be abandoned, and recommended two companies of cavalry be stationed there.[72]

On April 7, 1867, in pursuance of Special Order No. 13, from Headquarters United States Cavalry, Company G, the 4th United States Cavalry would reestablish Fort Chadbourne. They arrived on May 25, 1867. Following in June were Companies D, M, and A from Rio Concho and Fort Mason, and Company H arrived in July.

Immediately proposals were posted through newspaper advertisements to receive sealed bids for corn, hay, and all supplies needed for the Quartermaster's store, and to run a post.[73]

A permanent camp of one commissioned officer and fifty enlisted men from Fort Chadbourne, maintained a camp on a rotating basis on the main fork of the Concho River. This provided added protection on the frontier. Numerous other escorts for staff officers, mail, and trains were also furnished out of Fort Chadbourne.

The first Commander since the Federal troops were forced to leave Texas in 1861 was placed in command of Fort Chadbourne on May 1867. He was

Captain Eugene Beauharnais Beaumont of the 4th U. S. Cavalry.

Many officers, such as Captain Beaumont, moved their families along with them to the frontier. Captain Beaumont's wife and daughter resided here with him.

In June, while Captain Beaumont was away on a scouting trip, Margaret Beaumont, his wife, was home tending to her duties as wife and mother. The Beaumont's daughter Natalie was four years old at the time. As was the fashion in those days small children that could be out of sight in the blink of an eye were sometimes tethered to a stake, or picket pin. By today's standards this sounds somewhat outlandish. But, when you were on the frontier with the thought of your child wandering away, the scare of wild animals, or Indian attacks, you did this to protect your child. So occasionally they tied a long rope to the child, then to a stout stake. The child was able to play freely about the quarters, but could not wander off. It was all about safety.

Margaret had tied Natalie that day giving her approximately thirty feet to play. During this time there were usually herds of buffalo grazing a few miles from the fort, and since the reopening of the post they seemed to come nearer. During the last few years, when there were few soldiers stationed at the post, the buffalo had apparently taken a liking to the area, and sometimes used the parade grounds for grazing.

No one ever knew what spooked the large herd, but all of a sudden there was a rumbling noise heard across the grounds. At first everyone thought of thunder, but as the wall cloud of dirt grew, and their large shapes could be seen, it was evident it was a stampede of buffalo rushing towards the grounds.

Mrs. Beaumont was witness to the sound and ever approaching charge, but she was powerless to act; doing so she would also sacrifice her own life.

Lt. Peter Boehm who received the Medal of Honor for his actions during the Civil War, was stationed at Fort Chadbourne on this day. Seeing Natalie tied to the stake, and realizing the imminent danger approaching all of them, Lt. Boehm immediately ran for the little girl, picked her up into his arms, and headed for the only thing he thought might save their lives. A mesquite tree stood near the picket pin where she was tied. He pulled the pin, grabbed her up at the same time, and jumped into the small bushy tree clinging to it, while he protected the little girl in his arms. Desperately he clung to the tree, holding Natalie tight while the wild animals brushed against them as they passed. Boehm shouted and waved his arms as the buffalo parted to both sides of them. With what must have seemed like an eternity, the large animals finally passed them by. Both Natalie and Lt. Boehm were safe, and in all certainty Margaret was most grateful to the soldier who had saved her little girls life.[74]

Natalie Beaumont grew up and married Brigadier General George Alexander Forsyth. They had two children who died in infancy.

On July 26, 1867, a Board of Officers convened at Fort Chadbourne at 3 o'clock p.m. They included Captain E. B. Beaumont, 1st Lieutenant Theodore J. Wint, and 1st Lieutenant William C. Hemphill. The meeting was for the purpose of reporting upon the present condition of Fort Chadbourne as a six company post, with consideration to rebuilding the Fort, and discussing the scant supply and inferior quality of the water.

The board examined the state of the buildings, and concluded they were not habitable. Roofs needed new shingles, and most of the walls were breaking down. Their new plan included tearing down many of the old buildings in order to rearrange the grounds. Officers Quarters would be moved forward, and larger buildings for the enlisted men would need to be built. All wooden structures were deemed worthless.

In the end the board opposed reconstruction, and suggested the post be abandoned for the following reasons.

1. "No running stream near the post. Water is bad and must be hauled in wagons a distance up to one and one half miles. It smells offensively.

2. "A post for six companies of cavalry should only be established upon a running stream where there is sufficient good drinking and bathing water.

3. "Grass is of poor quality, scarce, and the soil is not favorable to its growth especially during dry seasons.

4. "No timber within a distance of forty miles

5.   "The duty for which the troops
        stationed here are called upon to
        perform, at the fork of the Concho, has
        an abundance of wood and water."[75]

Even though there was strong evidence that this post would not sustain reoccupation or be rebuilt, August through November 1867, there was an average of ninety-nine citizens employed in the Quartermasters Department. This included a superintendent, engineers, sawyers, stone masons, quarrymen, carpenters, blacksmiths, lime burners, wheelwrights, cooks, and guides. With five companies of the Fourth U. S. Cavalry stationed here, Fort Chadbourne was now the second largest military post in Texas, only behind Fort Brown in Brownsville.[76]

As late as October 4, 1867, a new Post Chaplain, Thaddeus B. McFalls was appointed, and requested to report for duty at Fort Chadbourne. The appointment was signed by then Secretary of War, Ulysses S. Grant. The original document itself is a permanent part of the Fort Chadbourne Foundation's vast collection of historical documents.

So until a decision was reached concerning rebuilding or abandonment of Fort Chadbourne, it was the same day to day life that the soldiers endured. In the meantime, the challenges they faced were ongoing but by the end of 1867, Special Order No. 27 was issued. Through headquarters of the Fifth Military District in San Antonio, Texas, the establishments of three new posts were announced.

The first would be situated in the fork of the Main and North Concho Rivers, first to be called Camp Kelly after Major Michael J. Kelly, a Fort Chadbourne soldier who died of typhoid fever earlier in the year. The post would house six companies of cavalry, two companies of infantry, and later Camp Kelly would be renamed Fort Concho. It was located near present day San Angelo, Texas, in Tom Green County.

The second post would be built on the Clear Fork of the Brazos and named Fort Griffin, which would house four companies of cavalry, along with two companies of infantry. It was located in Throckmorton County, near present day Albany, Texas.

Last but not least, Fort Richardson was located near Jacksboro, Texas, in Jacks County, and would house six companies of cavalry, and two companies of infantry.[77]

Even though in late 1867, new posts were being added, others decommissioned and some revamped, as always, Indian troubles were still a nagging problem on the frontiers of Texas. The war was over, and life was once again returning to normalcy, but the same elements that were present in the antebellum time, still persisted in post war Texas.

Several men stationed at Fort Chadbourne were killed in skirmishes with Indians through the last months of 1867. Privates John Maroney, Daniel Wurm, and Hugh Collins were all killed in close proximity to Fort Chadbourne.

In a letter dated August 22, 1867, 1st Lt. Peter Boehm, 4th U. S. Cavalry, Fort Chadbourne, reported that Privates Maroney and Wurm, of Companies D and H, left the post on a scouting party. The next morning Boehm rode out from the post at approximately 3:00 a.m. Roughly forty miles from Fort Chadbourne, and in an area near Mountain Pass on the old Overland Mail Route, he found the bodies of the two Privates. They were scalped, horribly mutilated, and almost impossible to recognize. Boehm buried their bodies on the right side of the road and immediately returned to the post.   Both of these men were later exhumed, and were buried in the San Antonio National Cemetery.[78]

The third soldier, Private Hugh Collins, 4th U. S. Cavalry, Company A, was killed in the opposite direction of the other two men while he was scouting southwest of Fort Chadbourne, on the North Concho River.

Although records indicate that three of the soldiers who died or were killed in 1867, at or near Fort Chadbourne were exhumed and moved to other locations, no documentation has been located concerning exhumation of soldiers from earlier years. Of the thirty-one men listed as deceased on Fort Chadbourne post returns, twenty-one were killed or died of natural causes within the perimeter of the post, while the other ten were killed in other locations.   Of those soldiers, only three of the thirty-one men have been located.   John Clark died of yellow fever, and the other two, Maroney and Wurm, were killed by Indian's, all three in the year 1867.   It is believed that the soldier's who died at Fort Chadbourne prior to the Civil War still remain in the vicinity of the post. There is some speculation as to the area, and at some time in the future, plans are for a memorial to be placed in their honor.

Military personnel were not the only men in danger. Trail rides across this barren unsettled portion of Texas were becoming a daily passage in 1866 and 1867. Many of the famous trails mentioned today were named for the men that drove cattle across this country. Two men most famous for their conquest were Charles Goodnight and Oliver Loving, who established a trail known as the Goodnight-Loving Trail. Fort Chadbourne sits right alongside this famous trail.

These large herds of cattle and drovers were dependent on the protection of the military, and the frontier posts scattered along these trails. It is said that Charles Goodnight rode into the post soon after the fort was reoccupied in 1867, and requested a military escort from then Fort Chadbourne Commander, Captain E. B. Beaumont. He complained of Indian's that continually followed their procession, and in concern for his men and cattle, he hoped that Beaumont could spare enough men to deter any action that the Indians might have in mind. Post returns made mention during that same time frame, that Lt.

Peter Boehm left Fort Chadbourne with fifty men to scout, and protect cattle herders crossing the plains.

The year before, one of Loving's herdsmen had been brought to the Fort where only a small detachment of federal troops were encamped. The soldiers treated the man for an arrow wound to his shoulder following an Indian attack. Loving gave the young man a good horse and sent him to Fort Chadbourne for medical assistance in hopes of saving the young mans arm. While there he met another herder John Hittson, who was trailing the same route as Goodnight heading for New Mexico. Hittson was no stranger to Indian Territory. He had assisted in the rescue of Cynthia Ann Parker in 1860, and his future would be witness to the Warren Wagon Train Massacre.[79]

In the book "On the Border with Mackenzie" its author, Captain Robert Carter[80] mentions that Colonel Ranald Mackenzie began an expedition in the spring of 1871 from Fort Concho to Fort Richardson with Companies A & E of the 4th U. S. Cavalry. On their march from Fort Concho to Fort Chadbourne, he and his troops rode past a small peak in present day Coke County that he referred to as Mount Margaret.

Being born and raised in Coke County myself, I have driven by this 335 foot tall landmark on the east side of the county all my life, and as the story had been relayed to me many times, it was supposedly named for a young white girl that had been captured, killed by Indians, and buried atop the mountain.

I had never questioned that story, until I read Captain Carter's account. He said the mountain was named after Margaret Beaumont, the loving and devoted wife of the soldier's favorite Captain, E. B. Beaumont, and of course one of Fort Chadbourne's commanders. Actually this makes more sense to me. Considering Mackenzie and Beaumont served together for many years in this area, and traveled past this mountain many times on their scouting trips, it stands to reason that Captain Carter's explanation is far more plausible simply because his reference to this is in 1871; long before Coke County was actually formed from Tom Green County, and its communities were built.

Colonel Mackenzie and his troops arrived that spring at Fort Chadbourne to find it abandoned except for some prairie dogs and buffalo grazing on the parade ground. A corporal and three privates guarding the mail station were the only military occupying the post.

Although there is a number of post returns through 1868, correspondence, newspaper clippings, and several memoirs concerning rendezvous through old Fort Chadbourne even as late as 1874, the post was considered officially abandoned long before that. That same year the Honorable W. W. Belknap, Secretary of War, wrote to the president of the Texas and Pacific Railroad Company on June 15, 1874, "I have the honor to inform you that the exact latitude and longitude, of Forts Chadbourne and Phantom Hill are not known in this Department". In other words Fort Chadbourne was no longer on the map.

Fort Chadbourne had served its purpose for many years, but lack of water and supplies demanded the military to find a more favorable location. Perhaps all those years later General John Garland was looking down saying "I told you so!"

Chapter XIII

The Horse Race

A fort built in the middle of nowhere will still attract a certain amount of individuals willing to cash in on its existence. Even soldiers on the frontier had a pay day, so sutler stores and saloons popped up almost as soon as posts were established. Most of the time these establishments were located on the very outskirts of the fort's perimeter, and Fort Chadbourne was no different. The store here was approximately one-eighth mile southwest of the Fort.

Army regulations of 1821 created the position of the post sutler. A post council consisting of four officers supposedly set prices. The sutler paid a tax to the post at a rate of ten to fifteen cents per soldier present at the post each month. In 1849, the Secretary of War forbid post sutlers to sell "ardent spirits, or other intoxicating drinks", but in 1856 an inspector found sutler's Howard and Lane did indeed sell liquor at Fort Chadbourne.

No time could the sutler offer credit greater than half the soldier's pay. Three days before payday the sutler had to present a record of accounts against each soldier to the company commander.[81]

The first post sutler at Fort Chadbourne appeared to be Richard A. Howard, who also owned land in the area, and was a partner in Evans, Howard, & Co. in San Antonio. But within a few months time John Zirvas Leyendecker, who at one time was a clerk for Mr. Howard and Anton Friedrich Wolff, filed an agreement for Leyendecker to open a mercantile business at Fort Chadbourne for trading with the Indians and soldiers. Wolff would purchase goods in Fredericksburg and freight them to Fort Chadbourne at a rate of $2.75 per 100 pounds. All profits, losses, and expenses would be divided equally between Leyendecker and Wolff.

The "Oak Creek Store", as it was listed on Bills of Lading in the Leyendecker Paper's, indicated items purchased were groceries, boots, shoes, and clothing. The summary of accounts showed several of the officers stationed here including a Fort Chadbourne

Commander, 2nd Lt. James Hawes, and Dr. Ebenezer Swift the assistant surgeon, had outstanding accounts. Another interesting tidbit was the fact that there was a listing with "Indian Accounts". Some interesting names pop up here including Chiefs Tecumseh and Sanaco; Guide, Sam Cherry; and Chief Mulaquetop. Mulaquetop was most likely the same Comanche Indian Chief whose tribe took part in the famous horse race at Fort Chadbourne between the soldiers here and the Indians.

There are several accounts of the horse race but the one Richard Dodge relates in his book "Thirty Three Years Among Our Wild Indians" was probably the most accurate one. Dodge served at Fort Chadbourne in 1853, and since the Leyendecker Bills of Lading place Mulaquetop around the Fort at the same time period, Dodge's would be the most acceptable of these legends.

Apparently Chief Mulaquetop and his band were frequent visitors to Fort Chadbourne. Although Dodge recalled them as nuisances and beggars, the officers enjoyed a friendly candor with them on occasion. One day the soldiers were badgering Chief Mulaquetop for a race, or perhaps it was the other way around.

Regardless, several of the officers owned blooded horses and challenged him against the third best horse of the garrison. The distance would be four hundred yards.

The Indians wagered robes and skins to a value of approximately seventy dollars against money, flour, sugar, etc. At the appointed time all the Indians and most of the garrison were assembled for the race. The Indians showed up with a miserable sheep of a pony, with legs like churns; a three inch coat of rough hair stuck out all over the body; and a general expression of neglect was evident. The rider was a brawny buck of one hundred and seventy pounds, looking big and strong enough to carry the poor beast he rode. He was armed with a huge club, which he used to strike the animal with from start to finish. To the astonishment of the entire garrison the Indian won by a neck.

Another race was proposed by the officers and after much dickering, it was accepted by the Indians. This time the race would be against the next best horse and the bets were doubled. In less than an hour the second race was run using the same Indian pony, with the same exertion and the exact same results. The soldiers lost!

The officers being thoroughly disgusted, proposed a third race and brought to the ground a magnificent Kentucky mare of the true Lexington blood, and known to beat the best of the other horses at least forty yards in four hundred. The Indians of course accepted the race, and not only doubled the bets, but piled up everything they could raise, seemingly crazed with the excitement of their previous success.

The riders mounted, the word was given. Throwing away his club the Indian rider gave a whoop at which time the sheep like pony pricked up his ears, and went running like the wind, almost two feet to the mare's one. The last fifty yards of the course was run by the pony with the rider sitting face to his tail, making hideous grimaces, and beckoning to the rider of the mare to come on.

Afterwards it transpired that the old sheep pony was a trick, and was a straight race pony. He was apparently celebrated among all the tribes of the south, and Chief Mulaquetop had only just returned from a visit to the Kickapoo in the Indian nation, who he had easily cleaned out of six hundred ponies.

I'm sure that day was a wonderful afternoon break from the monotony of military drills, long hours of manual labor, and a life that held few pleasurable moments for anyone on the frontier. I picture this day with military, civilians, women and children, lined up together cheering on this great adventure of a horse race between Indians and Soldiers. Everyone coming from their dusty tents, small huts, and work ceasing on the building of the Fort as word traveled around the post area of the great race taking place. For days and weeks after that, many a camp fire chat had to include the day the Indian Chief got the best of the soldier boys; and even after all these years the legend still lives on. Whether embellished or not, it had to be an exciting experience that day for all who stood on the sidelines of this momentous race!

The next few weeks had to seem dull and uneventful compared to that extraordinary day, because life on the frontier was one of survival, not fun. Even the approach of a freight wagon full of supplies, heading for the traders store or the Fort, had to be a welcome site to these isolated men and women.

Chapter XIV

Trade

There are many bills of lading, especially concerning the post sutler Leyendecker. As a trader, items were not only delivered to the post, but many articles collected or traded for were sent from the post to Fredericksburg or San Antonio.

For instance on October 4, 1853, Mr. Leyendecker sent to A. F. Wolff in Fredericksburg, fifty-eight bundles or five hundred forty-four pounds of dressed deer skins, six undressed deer skins, one half buffalo skin, fourteen lariats, one hair rope, fifty-four pairs of moccasins, two flint bags, and two hundred dollars in cash. Adam Radig received and signed for the items, then transported them to Fredericksburg.

During the year of 1854 alone there were a total of fifty-eight men listed as delivery men in Leyendecker's files, which makes one wonder that with all the supplies and cash going back and forth, how many problems arose.

At one time the trade between Jas R. Sweet and Company and John Leyendecker was tense because Sweet felt shorted for his corn deliveries. He apparently was owed more than twenty three hundred dollars from the Oak Creek Store at Fort Chadbourne, and Wolff had been promising the amount for some time, yet none had been received. Sweet expressed his disappointment in this way of doing business. He feared there would be no money left for him, and he insisted on being paid immediately.[82]

There was also trade with Indians and those stationed at the post. Eliza Holloway, wife of Fort Chadbourne Quartermaster Edmunds Holloway wrote letters and poetry while stationed at Fort Chadbourne. Many described the opportunities for trade with the Indians. Through her correspondence one can visualize life on a remote frontier post and ascertain how her day to day life among the military soldiers, and the marauding Indians became an almost natural part of her daily existence.

Although Eliza and Edmunds looked forward to trade with the Indians, because of the very unique items they offered, they were put off by their mischief making and thievery. Items stolen from them or other residents of the post would later show up being worn or bartered by one Indian or another.

Eliza lost two night caps that were hung on a line to dry. She explained that Chief Buffalo Hump later offered them back for trade. A large silver spoon stolen from the Post Commander's wife, Mrs. Beardsley, was converted into earrings and worn into the garrison by one of Indians. But Eliza, always hoping for special items to send home to relatives, endured some of the Indians wicked ways in order to trade for articles she desired for family members back east, such as the prized shell earrings she had sent her sister.

Other prized items were Indian headdresses with beads and long tails of feathers hanging down the back. Although not the one she had hoped for, Eliza told her mother she was able to acquire from Chief Yellow Wolf a "terribly ugly" headdress with horns that he explained "was good to scare the Mexican's in battle." From Chief Sanaco, she collected "picture writing."[83]

Eliza also spoke of how her husband Edmunds amused the old "Medicine Man" of the tribe by showing him pictures in books. She writes, "The old doctor often insists on having the picture cut out for him."

Although the residents at Fort Chadbourne were less than enthusiastic about the Indian's continued excursions into the post, they accepted some bad with the good, in order to bargain for their goods. Trade was an important part of survival for some, for others, a way to acquire unique souvenirs for family and friends, and pass the time of day.

In Eliza's July 24, 1853, letter sent from Fort Chadbourne, she explained to her Mom that she had tried unsuccessfully to purchase flower seed from the sutler. She wanted her mother to send her some touch-me-nots and portulaca seeds such as the pretty ones they had grown when she was at home.

Eliza tried to make the best of this desolate frontier life, and built a home for them regardless of the uncomfortable conditions she faced every day. She spent her days making jelly from wild plums, and pickles from watermelon rind. In one correspondence she mentioned a tea party she and some of the other officer's wives, had put together ending the evening with a grand dance held in honor of her visiting cousin Charles.

It was women like Eliza that aided in the survival of many of the men stationed at posts such as Fort Chadbourne. Her nurturing nature, her ability to build a home wherever her family was stationed, added much to the daily life at these frontier posts.[84]

Along with the sutler's store near the post, which today would be considered a local convenience store, and the individual trading that took place between soldier, Indian, and civilian, there was a Quartermaster at the Fort. He ordered, and organized, all the necessary supplies it took to feed the soldiers, and provide for the animals along with any other provisions needed to keep the establishment functioning. This included hiring civilians and extra duty men.

Bids were received through the Quartermaster for beef, corn, sugar, hay, etc. The price submitted was usually by pounds, tons, or bushels and this price included delivery transportation to the Fort.

As mentioned, an early Quartermaster was 1st Lt. Edmunds Balard Holloway, 8th U. S. Infantry. The first correspondence found from him was in soliciting a bid for beef at Fort Chadbourne. The winning bid went to Mr. L. Vandever for his proposal of four dollars and seventy cents per hundred pounds. A contract was made with him, because not only did he submit the cheapest bid, but he was also known to be very reliable. Reliability was a great incentive, just to know the product would actually arrive at the Fort. Hay was also a contract item, and delivered at eight dollars and forty-five cents per ton.

The majority of supplies for the forts were ordered from the San Antonio Depot. Independent of the post, seventy two wagons belonged to the depot and were driven by citizen teamsters employed in transporting supplies from the coast at Indianola, Texas, via San Antonio, and then to the frontier posts thereon; Fort Chadbourne being the greatest distance for delivery.

In the year of 1853, the average cost for the 8th military department from Indianola, Texas, to San Antonio, was one dollar and fifteen cents per hundred pounds; and onward to Fort Chadbourne one dollar and forty three cents for the same amount of weight.

Labor cost amounted to two thousand seven hundred and sixty five dollars, which covered payments of clerks, storekeepers, mechanics, laborers, teamsters, herders, cooks, etc. Monthly purchases accumulated to almost six thousand dollars, with quarterly disbursements of over fourteen thousand dollars.

In 1855, a wagon freight contract went to George T. Howard for moving army supplies in lots up to two hundred fifty thousand pounds on fifteen days notice, from the San Antonio depot to the Texas Forts, including Fort Chadbourne. Failure to deliver these supplies resulted in a fine of three dollars per day for each thousand pounds. Mr. Howard was also required to post a bond of more than a hundred thousand dollars.[85]

A report by James Belger, Quartermaster, San Antonio, to Major General Thomas S. Jessup, explained the route to these military forts quite well. From San Antonio to Fort Chadbourne via Fredericksburg and Fort Mason, was a distance of two hundred fifteen miles. This route used the road to Fort McKavett as far as Fort Mason, which was one hundred miles from San Antonio. From there to the San Saba River was 20 miles, over a rough and hilly road. This river was sometimes swollen, which could detain a train for two or three days. Next on the route was nineteen miles to Pecan Creek, which was a good watering place, then six miles to Brady's Creek, then on to the Concho River which was twenty seven miles. This river was always fordable. From there it was sixteen miles to the Colorado River, which occasionally rose so as to be impassable for days, but only after very heavy rains in the winter and spring. At all other times it was easily crossed. From there it was twenty seven miles to Fort Chadbourne. This country was always a good road to travel and afforded the best of grass and water during the spring, summer, fall and most of the winter season. However, there was no cover found between Forts Mason and Chadbourne."[86]

Chapter XV

Assistant Surgeon

Ebenezer Swift

Ebenezer Swift served at Fort Chadbourne from 1852-1856, as Assistant Surgeon and Meteorologist. He has always held a great interest to me, and always one of my favorites to refer to when an anecdote of the time period is needed. Perhaps it was because he was a very meticulous record keeper that makes it easy for research, or that he wrote a great many letters to his family, and to the military. He left his legacy at Fort Chadbourne, and in doing so he recorded many of the historical legends associated with this post.

Dr. Swift was born in Wareham, Massachusetts, October 8, 1817, to a very military oriented family beginning with their participation in the Revolutionary War. Eben Swift, as he penned his name on all official military documents, was the first of the Swift family to serve on the frontier known as Texas. He was the fifth son of Ezra and Lucy Swift. He enlisted in the United States Army as an assistant surgeon on October 30, 1847 during the Mexican War.

Much of the next few years found him stationed in Texas. His experience with the cholera epidemic in 1849, would eventually lead to his knowledge and treatment of the disease, in other areas of the country. On July 20, 1867, he was appointed brevet brigadier general for meritorious services voluntarily rendered during the prevalence of cholera at Fort Harker, Kansas.

On September 13, 1849, while assigned to the military post of Brazos Santiago, Texas, Dr. Swift witnessed the fury of a hurricane. He was awakened by a bright light flashing and the atmosphere seemed to be in flames. He said, "The hurricane lasted more than twenty minutes, and the ruin of the town was complete."[87]

In March 1851, Swift was ordered to Fort Martin Scott near present day Fredericksburg. During this time he met his wife to be, Sarah Edwards Capers. Many days he wrote to his sister exclaiming his love for Sarah. He said he was poor, and she had always been in the midst of affluence, surrounded by friends, gaiety and fashion, and that she was as lovely and pure as a snow flake. Sarah's visits to Fredericksburg became more frequent, and on February 18, 1852, he and Sarah were married.

March of that year, he was ordered to join the 8th United States Infantry, at a post in Indian Territory, some two hundred miles away, known as Camp Johnston. There his long stay on the military frontier would begin, as would his family life.

After only eight months at Camp Johnston, it was time again to move on, this time to Fort Chadbourne. On their trip from Camp Johnston, the easy life Sarah was accustomed to must have surely made her wonder what she had gotten herself into. Travel was never easy back then, and this day would certainly be no exception. The iron axle of the carriage they began their journey in broke, and they were forced to walk back four or five miles to camp. At this time Sarah was unable to ride horse back because she was with child.

Several days later after retrieving another carriage, the Swifts made their way to the new post without incident. They rode in on a cold day in early November, seeing a few tents, and little more. As of yet, the men had not had time to build accommodations, so for the next few months, even years, tents, huts, and lean-to's would have to suffice as home at Fort Chadbourne.

The Swift's accommodations were better than some, but less than Sarah was accustomed too. They lived in a tent 24x15 feet, divided by curtains to make several rooms. They had the whole tent furnished and nicely carpeted, but many days Sarah had to be homesick for the niceties she had grown up with during her childhood.

Mrs. Swift's brother, LeGrand Capers, had made the trip with them, as he was being instructed in medicine by Dr. Swift. Upon arrival LeGrand showed a great interest in starting a small fifty to sixty acre farm at the post. Much of his correspondence was with Mr. Leyendecker, in Fredericksburg, who would become the post sutler in a few months. LeGrand wanted to purchase oxen, ploughs, hoes, corn, potatoes, wagons, etc., and then find a trusting man who understood farming to help him with his agenda.

By February though, LeGrand must have changed his mind, and informed Mr. Leyendecker that it was late in the season. He had made a decision to forgo farming for the year. In the years to follow though, there was no mention of Mr. Capers ordering supplies, or seeds, for the purpose of farming. Even though he was non-military, maybe the issuance of General Order No. 3, by the War Department, on February 9, 1854, abolishing farming in the Army had something to do with it.

Perhaps having LeGrand here made it easier for Sarah to have a family member along that was non-military, and to be with her throughout the long days she must have faced at Fort Chadbourne. Although, in Dr. Swift's letters to his sister, Sarah who was from an affluent family, seemed to be portrayed as a very docile and delicate young lady. On the other hand, she had to be a much stronger, and tougher woman to survive day after day, living her husband's military life style at this desolate frontier fort.

She gave birth to three of his children at Fort Chadbourne. Sadly the first one born April 1853, died shortly after birth. The second one, Eben Swift was born on May 11, 1854, and the third, a boy LeGrand Capers Swift named after his Uncle, was born March 21, 1856.

Years later the second son, Eben Swift visited Fort Chadbourne to see the place of his birth. On August 18, 1917, he made his way to Sweetwater, Texas, by train and hired an automobile for ten dollars to take him to Fort Chadbourne. It took him two and one quarter hours to arrive at the old fort. He found Garland and Sallie Odom, second generation ranch owners, residing in the double officer's quarters, and assumed that the quarters next to this was the home he had lived in as a baby. By all reports this was not the correct assumption, because the Swifts had never resided in any of rock structures while at Fort Chadbourne. Swift described the remaining buildings as rough dressed stone and partly in ruins.

In his personal memoirs concerning his birth he said, "I was a source of interest among the Indian squaws who came into the post to see a white baby. They called me Chiquito Medico which is Spanish for Little Doctor.

"This is a bright day for me; I had wanted for many years to visit the scene of the early happiness of my parents."

.

Chapter XVI

Thirteen Arrows

In June 1853, Dr. Swift appeared to be looking for bigger and better things than living in a tent at Fort Chadbourne. Dr. Swift wrote to Brigadier General T. Lawson, the Surgeon General U.S.A., in Washington, D. C., offering his services as an Assistant Surgeon for the survey of the railroad route to the Pacific. Apparently the request was denied, because Dr. Swift continued to be stationed at the Fort long after this time.

When reviewing Dr. Swift's records and correspondence you find wonderful notes and detailed information concerning many day to day activities, whether it was medical, meteorological, or sometimes personal.

For instance, his sick and wounded reports each quarter let us in on not only soldiers who were ill, but a list in general of women and children who were sick or injured. He noted the number of cases he treated, their diagnosis and outcome, along with posting the arrivals or departures of all military companies on post. In other words, his data provides a wealth of information not found on reports furnished by other surgeons, or military personnel records of that time. As required by the Surgeon General's office, medical personnel had strict guidelines to follow, but Swift went beyond just filling in the blanks of a quarterly report, and in doing so added to the historical data we research today.

Some of his letters are short, but to the point. For example, in one letter dated March 18, 1854, Dr. Swift reported that oxen at the post had been stolen by the Indians, and he had sent scouts out to retrieve the oxen. In another note to the U. S. Surgeon General in Washington, D. C., he complained that the Comanche Indians kept stealing his rain gauge.

Now, this has been debated many times, especially around Fort Chadbourne as to why and what the Indians would want with a rain gauge. The idea has been tossed the idea around, and most conclude that the Comanches saw Dr. Swift go out to the rain gauge after there had been measurable precipitation. Evidently they presumed that the gauge itself, held some mysterious properties, and that it was the rain gauge itself that actually made the rain fall from the sky. There is no certified documentation per say on this, but that idea does make sense.

A frontier military physician, such as Dr. Swift, faced many varied diseases and injuries. During his tenure here, a new Fort was being built, so everyday contusions and fractures were prevalent, and even more serious type injuries were recorded. Digestive disorders, constipation and diarrhea, were always widespread, along with the usual rheumatism, common colds, bug bites, and poison vines. Cholera was common due to unsanitary practices and contaminated water. There were cases of Tuberculosis, even a case of Smallpox was communicated on one report concerning a Comanche with Sanaco's band. Swift noted that the disease spread no farther than the one incidence. Care of civilians, including women and children were also a part of his itinerary. Venereal diseases such as syphilis and gonorrhea were not uncommon among the soldiers, scurvy occurred when fruits and vegetables were in short supply, even drunkenness was a drawback, and then of course there were problems associated with injuries from weapons.

Several occurrences of this happened at Fort Chadbourne including an accidental shooting of a soldier shot by a sentinel. Private Gilbert Martin, 1st U. S. Infantry, Company F, was shot and killed one night when the sentinel on duty mistakenly took him for an Indian. This occurred the very next night after Indians had tortured and mutilated the mail carriers. It is probable the private on duty was nervous, and shot at the first sound he heard in the dark.

Dr. Swift treated some of his friends too. Mr. Leigh and Billy Green, who went hunting for panthers, got into what today we'd likely describe as poison ivy. Seems Mr. Leigh grabbed a hold of the poisonous vine while on the trip, causing his face and eyes to swell shut. But the good news, they killed three panthers, one measuring eight and a half feet from nose to end of tail![88] Panthers are not normally prevalent to this area.

Dr. Swift met many challenges before and after his days at Fort Chadbourne, but one of the most famous stories connected with Fort Chadbourne was documented by Dr. Swift on the December 31st, 1854, sick and wounded quarterly report. The actual event took place on September 6, 1854. Why this occurrence was not listed on the September report is unclear, but apparently Dr. Swift waited until he knew the final outcome before recounting it on the end of year records.

In his own words and handwriting it reads: "On the night of the sixth of September last Private Matlock of Company F 2nd U. S. Dragoons sustained thirteen arrow wounds. An arrow which passed through his leg and two others he had removed before coming to the hospital. He then had six sticking in his back; one of which entered left of the spine and passed out an inch below the right nipple; two thus entered the cavity of the thorax and two the abdomen; one of the latter entered the right side entered five inches. Air issued from the wounds of the chest and blood from the mouth. He was bled copiously cupped and purged and was subsequently sustained with Quinine Wine and a nutritious diet. He has sufficiently recovered to be put to ordinary light duty in his company."[89]

2nd Lt. David S. Stanley, 2nd U. S. Dragoons, was stationed here on the night the attack transpired. In his personal memoirs he described the night as beautiful, bright, and moonlit. He and Lt. George B. Anderson were sleeping in one room of the hospital when they were awakened by a strange noise. They found Private Ruben Matlock being carried by another soldier and his wife. Matlock had been across Oak Creek, in the vicinity of the Hog Farm Saloon. There he had partaken in an over abundance of liquor, and on his way home, while crossing the creek, was attacked by several Comanche Indians. He had been able to make his way to the soldier's cabin. The soldier then brought him to Dr. Swift at the hospital.

Stanley called it an incredible sight. The arrows in Matlock bristled like a porcupine. Three of the arrows had gone so far through him that Dr. Swift had to extract them by cutting off the feathered part and pulling the arrows through the mans body. Amazingly his only disability was from a superficial wound which had lacerated a nerve, and gave the young soldier a slight limp the rest of his life.

Stanley wrote, "Assistant Surgeon Eben Swift who treated this man said he feared a truthful relation of the case would result in his being put down as a Munchausen."

Lt. Stanley explained that his whole point of relating the story was to show that arrow wounds do not compare with those made by bullets in fatality.

Years later Dr. Swift's son noted that his father had kept the arrows with him for many years as a souvenir from that day, but they had later been destroyed in a fire.

In 1870, Dr. Swift filed a lawsuit against Hannibal Railroad and St. Joseph Railroad Company, for a fire that had taken place in 1861. The Swift's sued for five thousand nine hundred and fifty eight dollars in lost baggage, and personal property owned by them. The railcar in which the items were stored for travel had burned and everything inside was a total loss.

In December 1861, almost all of the St. Joseph, Missouri, area was in a state of rebellion against the United States, and numerous times the railroad was ambushed by rebels. On demand of the commanding officer of the troops, the railroad had to furnish transportation for the troops, their baggage, arms, munitions, etc., but the railroad refused to make any contract for the transportation due to the danger along the line, especially in the region from St. Joseph to Hannibal.

On this day, Eben and Sarah were riding on the train with the rest of the garrison from Fort Randall to Cincinnati, Ohio. A surgeon was allowed eight hundred pounds of baggage, but Swift estimated his goods to be approximately twenty-seven hundred pounds. They listed furniture, silverware, buffalo robes, mattresses, desks, engravings, pictures, and jewelry, along with a set of surgical instruments and an unpublished manuscript on veterinary care of horses, which he had worked on for five years. All the items were placed inside a railcar, and then locked because it also carried nine thousand musket cartridges. Since the car was secured in this way, they were unable to save any of the items when the fire broke out.

Although the arrows in question were not specifically listed in the lawsuit, the fact that his son relates the loss of the arrows in a fire, leads one to believe that this was indeed the incident of loss.

The railroad in their defense did not believe they should be held responsible. They stated that the plaintiff had chosen to place his items in the car chosen by the commanding officer, along with the military equipment. But if by choice, Dr. Swift could have placed his personal items in the regular baggage car, leaving it in charge of the railroad's baggage master. The only car on the train attacked and burned was indeed the car with the Swift's effects, and the military munitions. All passenger and railroad baggage cars were unscathed.

When the judgment was handed down in 1870, the Swift's were only awarded one thousand dollars for the worth of the manuscript, but the judge added six per cent interest for the eight years that had elapsed since the fire. This brought the total assessment to six thousand five hundred thirty seven dollars and fifty cents. The railroad appealed the case to the Supreme Court which upheld Swift's award on November 20, 1871, ten years after the fire.[90]

It is certain Ebenezer Swift, David Stanley, and George Anderson, enjoyed telling this unbelievable account of being awakened in the night to see a soldier looking like a porcupine. But, Private Ruben Matlock himself must surely be the one that adlibbed his own rendition to his children and grandchildren, how he was shot full of arrows one day, while fighting the

Comanche, and lived to tell about it. Whether he admitted to being ambushed while inebriated, it is doubtful, but holding his grandson in awe while recounting the tall tale, had to be a thrill to the veteran soldier in his old age.

One thing disconcerting in military record keeping was the way the enlisted men of that time were documented, or should I say undocumented. They are found on muster rolls, post returns, etc., but seldom was there any documentation to take you much farther than that they existed, and were paid approximately every four months. If you were a private in the 1850's, it was almost as though you did not exist. There was much data on all officers of that time period, but enlisted men were apparently dispensable when they joined the military.

Tracing Private Ruben Matlock would be challenging, and I have tried, but with no luck in finding the information I seek.

Chapter XVII

Other Medical Personnel

The year of 1854, at Fort Chadbourne, kept Dr. Swift busy. It ended with an injury to Private John Mirror, 2nd U. S. Dragoons, Company G. On the morning of December 15th, Mirror was driving mules attached to a mill grinding corn. He fell from the board in the center of the large iron cog, between the phalanges and ground, crushing his leg just above the ankle. Dr. Swift put the patient under with chloroform and amputated his leg four inches below the tubercle of the tibia, and dressed it. The stump did not heal satisfactorily and gangrene set in. The gangrenous part was sprinkled with Quinoa, and Private Mirror was given Brandy, Quinine, and Morphine by mouth. The following morning he was greatly improved, and he recovered without incident. In May 1855, the soldier was medically discharged.[91]

Post Surgeons were required to wear many hats. Dr. Swift was also an Ornithologist. Much of his time spent at Fort Chadbourne was used to research and document many of the birds that were native to the area. His findings were acknowledged in the 1942 Edition of Ornithologists of the United States Army Medical Corps by Edgar Erskine Hume. Swift collected certain birds and sent them to Professor Spencer F. Baird at the Smithsonian (1850-1900), who in return wrote reports for the Pacific Railroad Survey. The partial list of species found at Fort Chadbourne, packaged and sent to Professor Baird were: the Road Runner, Western Night Hawk, Fork-tailed Flycatcher, Long-tailed Chat, Barn Swallow, Bell's Vireo, Mocking Bird, Summer Red Bird, Lark Finch, Yellow-headed Blackbird, Orchard Oriole, Carolina or Common Dove, and the Killdeer.[92]

Even though Dr. Swift was busy with other things at Fort Chadbourne, besides his duties as a doctor, by 1856 he had had enough of this frontier fort. He wrote Brigadier General Thomas Lawson, the Surgeon General of the United States Army, and requested to be relieved from duty at Fort Chadbourne.

The jest of the letter confirmed the remoteness of the post. He wrote that few civilians ever stopped by besides the beef contractor and a whiskey salesman. He or his family had not been off the post since their arrival in 1852, and there wasn't even satisfactory reading or study possibilities, which he felt would hamper his advancement as a doctor.

He added that sometimes there were no more than two or three officers present at the Fort besides himself, and at one time he was left in command of the post with only two companies of U. S. Dragoons.

He and his family had resided in tents for two years. At the time of his request for transfer, at their own expense, they live in two log pens and a passage covered in part by canvas, which was totally inadequate in protection from the wet and cold.

He added that food was also inadequate, and with the failure of gardens three out of the four years they had resided at Fort Chadbourne, he professed there was not even vegetables to eat.

In the end he wanted a better position for himself and his family and he felt he had done his duty on the frontier. He deserved better, and he wanted out of this hell hole of Texas.

In March, Dr. Swift finally received a reply informing him that as soon as a medical officer became available he would be relieved of his duty at Fort Chadbourne. Headquarters assumed one would be available by June 1st. Swift quickly replied that he would like to be relieved sooner than that. With permission he would hire a citizen at his own expense, in order to move his family by the middle of May. He had grave concerns for his wife and children being at the Coast and New Orleans in what he described as "the sickly period of the year." He did not wish to expose them to the epidemics, and he did not want to be stuck at this post another year.

Finally by Special Order 57 issued from Headquarters, Department of Texas, Assistant Surgeon Elisha P. Langworthy arrived at Fort Chadbourne to relieve Dr. Swift.

On June 7, 1856, Ebenezer and Sarah Swift along with their two young sons departed Fort Chadbourne in a small carriage headed for San Antonio. Sarah and Eben would never lay eyes on this post again, but one son would return. The day they said their goodbyes was the same day that the Indians who murdered the mail carriers rode into the Fort and were killed, wounded, and arrested on the parade grounds of the post.

Out of concern for the Swifts, later in the day Captain Seth Eastman sent out an escort to warn them of the increased danger and see that they made their way safely to San Antonio, which they did without incident.

Dr. Ebenezer Swift served the rest of his life in the Army. In 1880 his beloved wife Sarah passed away in New York. In 1884 Swift remarried a woman half his age, Clara P. Wilder, and on December 24, 1885, Ebenezer Swift died while stationed in Hamilton, Bermuda at the rank of General. The second Mrs. Swift lived until 1919.

Besides Dr. Swift, Fort Chadbourne had a number of Assistant Surgeon's serve at this post.

The doctor that finally gave Swift his freedom from frontier duty; Elisha P. Langworthy was a native of New York and graduated from Geneva College. He applied for an assistant surgeon position in the United States Army in 1849, and found his way to Texas in 1855, proceeding on to Fort Chadbourne in 1856. He resigned from service in 1860.

Like Ebenezer Swift, William Wallace Anderson was also an Ornithologist for the United States Army Medical Corps. Anderson was born in 1824 in South Carolina. His earliest presence in Texas was 1849. He was assigned to Fort Chadbourne on September 27, 1860, and arrived on October 16, 1860.

One of his bird sketches, the Blue-headed Flycatcher is found in the same edition as Swifts contributions to the book mentioned earlier. He was also known to sketch many of the forts where he was stationed. In locating the name of his granddaughter residing in Ohio, who was listed in the Ornithology book published in 1942, I tried to locate some remaining family that would know of theses sketches in hopes of finding a Fort Chadbourne likeness. I contacted several people in the Gates Mills community, along with the historical society there, and although I was unable to find any further information, I was told many of Dr. Anderson's sketches and any information the historical society had possessed were stored in a basement, and all had been lost due to a flooding in that facility.

It is sad that much of both Swift's and Anderson's research collected through the years was lost due to fire or flood.

Upon arrival to Fort Chadbourne, Dr. Anderson contacted the Surgeon General of the United States Army concerning his wife and children. Shortly after returning to Texas from North Carolina, Anderson faced the loss of a son, and was anxious to rejoin with his family. He wanted to bring them to Texas to be with him, but did not want to put them through the perils of travel unless he was to be permanently stationed in Texas for the next few years. He was willing to serve his next tour here, and was willing to forgo leaves of absence if he could be guaranteed the next four or five years service in Texas, with his family by his side. He wanted to wait until Chaplain Michell, who was at that time on leave due to the death of his own son, returned, and then apply for a leave of absence for sixty days and move his family to Texas. This never transpired. In a few short months Fort Chadbourne would be in the hands of the Texas Regimental Forces and Dr. Anderson would be on his way back East, not to retrieve his family, but to face the outbreak of the Civil War.

Assistant Surgeon William Babcock began his frontier service here in 1858, and less than a year later transferred from this post. In October 1859, Babcock died. According to his father, William had grown weak, thin, and feeble when he visited him at Fort Belknap. William attributed his failing health to exposure encountered while on a scouting trip with Major Earl Van Dorn, and having to live in tents which provided little protection from cold and rain.

Assistant Surgeon William Amos Carswell arrived 1859. Carswell graduated from medical college in South Carolina, where he was Assistant Demonstrator of Anatomy, and Prosector to the Professor of that branch of Science. In July 1857, he signed a contract with Surgeon General Thomas Lawson agreeing to perform the duties as an Assistant Surgeon in the United States Army. He was paid one hundred dollars a month.

Dr. Charles Henry Smith first saw military service in 1847, during the Mexican War. After serving in Florida, he was back in Texas, and stationed at Fort Mason from 1856 to 1859. When that post was abandoned, Smith went to Camp Cooper, and then served at Fort Belknap until its abandonment, later arriving at Fort Chadbourne. While stationed at the post he applied to the Army Medical Board for an examination for promotion, and it was granted. He left for New York in April 1860, leaving the post chaplain Tobias Michell to serve as physician in his absence until another assistant surgeon could be sent to Fort Chadbourne. Michell agreed to perform these duties free of charge until September, or until a new medical officer could relieve him. In June, Chaplain Michell received sad news of his son's death. Under the circumstances the chaplain's request for leave without delay was granted, which left Fort Chadbourne without medical assistance. Dr. William Morrow was soon directed to the post to serve until Dr. William Wallace Anderson arrived in October.

At the arrival of the Texas Mounted Rifles to Fort Chadbourne in 1861, Jesse A. Dereson, age 30, served as Surgeon aided by Private Lane who served as the hospital steward. On May 9, 1861, Doctor Dereson was mustered into Captain Sidney Green Davidson's Company of the Confederate States Army. Other than the mention of Dereson and Lane found on the Company muster roll, there is very little information concerning hospital personnel during the Civil War time period at Fort Chadbourne.

The last doctor that would serve at Fort Chadbourne was Conrad C. Dumreicher. He was born in Germany in 1838. He was assigned to the Illinois Volunteers, 1st U. S. Cavalry in 1862, and later ordered to report to San Francisco, California. He served in Washington Territory, promoted to Surgeon of Volunteers, and remained in the northwest until 1864, when he was arrested for insubordination. He was acquitted after a trial and mustered out of the service in 1865. In 1866, he received Special Order 271, sending him to the Department of Texas for duty. While attached to the 4th United States Cavalry, he was sent to Fort Chadbourne, and remained there until its abandonment in 1867.

An incident concerning a well respected officer at Fort Chadbourne, Major Michael J. Kelly and his death from typhoid fever, would lead to a court martial of Dumreicher. On August 13, 1867, officers at Fort Chadbourne brought charges against the doctor accusing him of being so drunk that he was unable to properly perform his duties as post surgeon. Dumreicher had been nicknamed by the men as "Hog" because as they said he "talks so simple and is such a drunkard."[93]

In September 1867, Captain E. B. Beaumont sent a letter to the Chief Medical Officer, of the District of Texas, concerning the ability of Dr. Dumreicher. The letter is as follows: "We the undersigned officers of the 4th U. S. Cavalry, most respectfully request that Assistant Surgeon C. C. Dumreicher, U. S. Army, be relieved from duty at this Post. We make the request for the following reasons; that we entertain a serious doubt as to his professional ability; that we place no confidence in him as a physician; that the enlisted men of this command distrust him and shrink from entering the Post Hospital for this cause; that diseases are making their appearance at this time and we look forward with dread in case an epidemic should break out at the Post.

"Entertaining the distrust that we do, we feel it only our duty to take this unpleasant and unusual method of appealing to the Medical Director believing that the necessity of the case warrants such procedure. We therefore respectfully request that Assistant Surgeon C. D. Dumreicher be removed and that one or more Surgeons be sent to this Post at once."[94]

That very same month, C. C. Dumreicher wrote to Bvt. Major General G. L. Hartsuff at the Military District, New Orleans, LA., concerning a charge placed against 1st Lt. Thomas J. Wint of the 4th U. S. Cavalry for conduct unbecoming an officer. On or about the morning of May 3, 1867, Dumreicher charged that Wint had made a personal assault by striking him on the parade ground at Fort Mason. Dumreicher stated he had waited until now to complain giving Lt. Wint the opportunity to apologize. He made clear Lt. Wint had sent a written apology under duress from another officer, but Wint continued to affront him at every opportunity. He further stated that on the evening of the 24th of September 1867 Lt. Wint once again without provocation insulted him in front of the Fort Chadbourne Commanding Officer's tent in the presence of several other officers.

Army records show Dumreicher was dismissed from service on June 17, 1868, and by 1875 Conrad Carl Dumreicher was an inmate at Mercy Hospital in Chicago, Illinois.

Chapter XVIII

Butterfield Stage Station

The Butterfield Trail ran right smack through historic Fort Chadbourne. Although nothing is mentioned concerning this Stage Stop in the military records that were researched, it had to be a thrill every time the soldiers heard the toot of the stagecoach horn signally its arrival. It must have boosted morale, at least for a few short minutes, and caused these tired and weary soldiers to feel less isolated, and not totally banished to a forgotten wasteland. The Butterfield Stage Stop became a part of their lives, and in return the Stage Stop was well protected in its close proximity to the military post.

The Stage Stop was built one hundred feet north of the enlisted men's barracks using the same sandstone as that used on the military buildings. It consisted of five rooms, three fireplaces, a cedar roof, and wood floors. There was a corral at one end. An archeological excavation in 2008 answered many of the questions pertaining to this particular building, and restoration of the stage stop was completed in November 2009.

Numerous accounts and books have been written about the Butterfield Overland Mail. Probably the most read was the account of the first through passenger on the west bound stage who was a correspondent for the New York Herald, Mr. Waterman B. Ormsby. Yes, the Butterfield was part of the story of this historic Fort, but rather than go into another long monologue of what many other historians have already written time and again, this book will simply touch on the main highlights of its beginning, and the interesting stories that emphasize its legendary tales through Fort Chadbourne.

By Act of Congress in 1857, John Butterfield was awarded the contract which would become the Butterfield Overland Mail Route. On September 16, 1857, Butterfield signed a six year contract at six hundred thousand dollars per annum for semi weekly service, between St. Louis, Missouri, and San Francisco, California.

In September 16, 1858, the first stage left St. Louis, Missouri, where Mr. Ormsby began his great journal to the world concerning his transcontinental passage. It was a grueling trip, day and night, riding through rain and cold, dust and heat, Indian attacks and just the day to day grind of broken wheels and wild mules.

The stage arrived for the very first time at Fort Chadbourne on September 23, 1858. In a matter of one week the stage had driven nine hundred and fifty-five miles. It pulled into Fort Chadbourne to the whoops and hollers of the 2nd U. S. Dragoons, Company G, commanded by Captain William Bradfute. One can see these young men running out of the barracks and across the parade ground to welcome this historic first. There had to be cheers, pats on the back, smiles, and laughter, as these men surrounded the stagecoach with its lone passenger and driver. Even the few women and children that were part of life on this post had to be racing at high speed to see its grand appearance. Finally the Butterfield Overland Mail had arrived at Fort Chadbourne, and there was something new to see and talk about. This meant the fort would now have more contact with the outside world through its passengers, letters, and newspapers. While the post was still physically isolated, it was no longer totally isolated from what was happening across the country.

The schedule for the West bound stage departed the Fort every Tuesday and Friday at 3:15 p.m. (See Fig.5) Even with today's travel seldom are we right on time. We consider a few minutes late, part of the deal. But how in the world considering the terrain, the weather, the breakdowns, and Indian attacks, did one actually arrive or depart on time, riding in a stagecoach? It is a given it did not happen that often, but the Butterfield did their best to keep to the tight schedule. The East bound stage left Fort Chadbourne every Wednesday and Saturday at 1:15 a.m. That stage was probably not met with the same excitement as the initial arrival, but interest probably continued for no other reason than it broke the tedium and monotony of daily life on the frontier.

After leaving Fort Chadbourne, the stage had the grueling task of heading for El Paso along the thirty second parallel, one of the longest and most desolate parts of the route.

On his arrival at Fort Chadbourne, Mr. Ormsby spoke of there being very few houses besides the government buildings, and few inhabitants but the soldiers. Dr. Swift had spoken of the same thing in his last year at the post. Total isolation!

One thing interesting Ormsby does relate to in his feedback, was the presence of a barricade that surrounded Fort Chadbourne, supposedly built a few years earlier in anticipation of Indian attacks. No where in military records, inspection reports, or correspondence was there ever any mention of a barricade encircling this fort, or even considered at Fort Chadbourne. In all recollections the stage went sweeping into the Fort, Indians rode into the Fort, horses raced across the parade ground, buffalo's stampeded, but not one other time do we ever find anything that would lead us to believe there was this barricade Ormsby points out in his article. Of all the years on Chadbourne Ranch, the family, and the many cowboys that have ridden its range, nothing has been found believed to be a part of this barricade. Fort Chadbourne does not confer with Mr. Ormsby on this aspect of his report.

The stagecoach associated with Fort Chadbourne was a Celerity wagon pulled by mules; a heavier duty wagon, with canvas flaps for doors and windows. Most people think of the Concord when they picture a Stagecoach, a somewhat fancier contraption with actual doors and small canvas windows, but the Celerity or "mud wagon", was the one mainly used on the route through Fort Chadbourne. It was usually pulled by mules instead of horses.

Mr. Ormsby said he was delayed here because the wild mules had to be caught and harnessed. Mr. Wheeler was the station keeper at Fort Chadbourne, while J. B. Nichols was the stage driver. Mr. Mather, an employee of the Butterfield Overland Mail, rode ahead on horseback to point out the road on the initial run. Mr. Ormsby was never sure whether it was Mr. Nichols driving, or the fact that Mr. Mather rode at a high rate of speed, and Nichols tried to keep up with him, but the mules were wild and untamed. All the whooping and hollering of the soldiers could have also spooked them, but it took them what seemed like hours, to hook up the mules, and then travel the next few miles. Mr. Ormsby described the mules with every adjective available; they "reared, pitched, twisted, whirled, wheeled, ran, stood still, and cut up all sorts of capers." The Celerity performed so many evolutions that in fear of his life, Mr. Ormsby abandoned the stagecoach and decided to walk. He felt this was less of a risk than getting his neck broken while riding on the stage.

The sutler from the fort, like everyone else, wanted to be a part of this momentous event, and had saddled his horse and ridden out along side the stage. At the time he probably did not realize the show would be that good. Seeing Mr. Ormsby walking, he offered to let him ride behind him, and Mr. Ormsby though apprehensive, accepted. The stage kept gyrating, the mules got more tangled, and one mule finally managed to get loose and headed for the hills; then followed the complete demolition of the top of the stage, while those in charge of it lay around on the grass, tired and disgusted.

But, the driver Mr. Nichols did not give up. He found the mules, harnessed them up once more, and they were on their way. After all, the mail must go on. Through the years when Ormsby reminisced of his trip across the Wild West, more than likely he would always relate Fort Chadbourne to the place he first felt at the young age of twenty-three he should write his last will and testament.[95]

Found throughout research history gives you many conflicting stories. Some you can verify, some you are sure are half truths, and some are just tall tales. Either way it adds spice to the adventure, and entertains us along the way.

There is a story in several books which concerns the Fort Chadbourne Stage Stop, and a shoot out that occurred at not the famous OK Corral, but at the corral located at the east end of Fort Chadbourne's Butterfield Stage Stop. At a fundraiser in 2008, Fort Chadbourne celebrated the 150th Anniversary of the Butterfield Overland Mail, and Mr. Barry Corbin[96] starred as the station keeper, Mr. Wheeler. The story of the shootout was used as the backdrop.

It began with Dr. Tucker, a San Francisco physician who was on his way home. We can only imagine the travel then; twenty three days and nights, hot, sweating, dust clinging to everything you owned, sitting knee to knee, elbow to elbow with no room to move. If you were lucky the folks aboard were friendly and entertaining, or if you were unlucky you could end up with the worst of obnoxious, drinking, smoking, swearing travelers.

Dr. Tucker boarded the stage in St. Louis, Missouri, and struck up a conversation with a Texan who owned property in Texas. At one of the stage stops along the way, two women traveling with what appeared to be two French gamblers loaded up, along with a very unpleasant foul tempered, foul mouthed individual. Dr. Tucker realized then it was going to be a long ride. The apparently inebriated man continually complained about the conditions inside, while insisting on smoking a stinking pipe, even with the ladies on board.

Sometimes stagecoaches were extremely packed with travelers, and at times so much so, that passengers would be required to ride in between the two seats on the floor. Perhaps that is why the man was so obnoxious, due to his less than comfortable seating arrangement, but he finally dosed off leaning against the stage door. This brought on a round of loud and incessant snoring.

Now as Dr. Tucker remembers, the Texan reached around the sleeping man, slipped the latch on the door, and when the stage lurched its way along, the door flew open, and the fat, stinking man fell out to the ground below.

The stage halted, and the other passengers not knowing what else to do, tried to aid the fellow traveler. He became violent and accusing, and even yelled that someone had tried to murder him. After picking him up and dusting him off, the Texan tired of this mans incessant fuming personality would not allow him inside the coach, and banished him to ride in the rear boot of the stage.

That is where trouble began. One of the ladies traveling with the gamblers was very taken with the handsome Texan and how he had handled the situation. She began to show him much attention as they road along the trail. This made her traveling companion irately jealous, and the longer they rode, the angrier he became.

When they finally reached Fort Chadbourne and disembarked, the French gambler challenged the Texan to a duel. The Texan not one to back down from a fight, accepted. The Texan was allowed to choose his weapon of choice, and he chose revolvers. Dr. Tucker would act as his second, and the gambler's friend would fend for his buddy. They chose the corral located at the east end of the station, and entered from opposite sides.

Dr. Tucker recounted the event this way. "The riled passenger suddenly fired two shots. At the second discharge, the Texan half wheeled to the left and staggered. His exposed left arm was shattered near the wrist. He sprang forward and both men shot once again without hitting each other. Once again they fired and the only result was that the Texan's hat was knocked off. At this point the Texan dropped upon one knee, and resting his revolver across his wounded arm, fired with deliberate aim. Throwing his hands up in the air, the gambler fell dead.

"By this time the stage driver had eaten his supper, fresh horses were in harness and the Texan and I could only seize some food and jump into the coach as the six wild mustangs started off on a fierce gallop. I also carried off some shingles from Fort Chadbourne to splint the Texan's broken arm."[97]

The story continued years later when Dr. Tucker chanced upon the Texan once again. By this time, the Texan had a large spread, and was a wealthy cattle and land baron in Texas.

So was this story related to actual accounts? Some people like to argue it was a different stage stop altogether. It is doubtful it took place exactly this way. Dr. Tucker through the years, most likely enlivened his ride across the Wild West. His story though was mentioned in more than one account, and it says the shoot out between a Texan and a gambler was at Fort Chadbourne.

In the San Francisco Bulletin dated September 15, 1859, there is also reference to another gunfight at Fort Chadbourne that supposedly took place September 2, 1859. The article referred to the stage stop at Fort Chadbourne as Hardy's Station. Supposedly Ham, who at that time was acting as the station keeper, shot and killed one of the stage drivers whom they identified as a Mr. Lowe. As of the printing of the newspaper, no one appeared to know what caused the shooting. As of this writing there has been no further information found concerning this gunfight, or either of the men named in the shooting.

In 1859, Samuel Peter Heintzelman, who would later hold the rank of Major General for the Union Army during the Civil War, passed through Fort Chadbourne on the stage. Heintzelman owned two silver mines in Arizona, and was returning east with some ore samples to show his investors. He also had collected several items for the Smithsonian Institute, including shells and a dead snake.[98]

Traveling with him was Charles Schuchard, an engineer who had visited Fort Chadbourne in 1854, while accompanying the Andrew Belcher Gray survey crew. Schuchard also known for his wonderful art work, had painted a lithograph of Fort Chadbourne that is still available today. (See Fig. 6) The view appears to be drawn as Mr. Schuchard was sitting atop a hill southwest of the Post, looking northeast, with several fort buildings aligned in the sketch, and a navigational landmark known as Church Peak in the background. He also did a rendition of what he entitled, "Church Mountain Valley" near Fort Chadbourne that also depicts that same peak. The military road from Fort Chadbourne to Fort Phantom Hill passed this famous peak, and the Butterfield Overland Mail Stage used it for reference twice a week.

On January 24, 1865, much of Schuchard's work was lost in a Smithsonian Institute fire when a defective flue started a fire above the picture gallery.

The Butterfield Overland Mail was of short duration. After just three short years of operation, the outbreak of the Civil War ceased its route. The service from San Francisco to St. Louis was discontinued by an act of Congress which was approved on March 2, 1861. On June 20, 1861, the Butterfield Route, No. 12578 ceased service. The last east bound stage actually traveled through Fort Chadbourne on March 12, 1861. The last westbound stage which left Fort Smith in April, 1861, was blocked at Fort Chadbourne, and the end of the Butterfield Overland Mail across this area would be no more. The saga of the Butterfield Overland Mail and its association with Fort Chadbourne was over.

On October 12, 1930, Roscoe P. Conkling visited Fort Chadbourne, and made several sketches of the layout of the old Post, and the Butterfield Stage Stop. It wasn't until 1947, that Conkling finally published his years of work in a three volume set called, "Butterfield Overland Mail". It contained several photographs taken at Fort Chadbourne, including the Butterfield Stage Station, along with one of Mr. Conkling standing in front of the ruins of the West Barracks.

No. 1] [Sep. 16th, 1858.

OVERLAND MAIL COMPANY.

THROUGH TIME SCHEDULE BETWEEN

ST. LOUIS, MO., MEMPHIS, TENN. } & SAN FRANCISCO, CAL.

GOING WEST.

LEAVE.	DAYS.	Hour.	Distance, Place to Place.	Time allowed.	Av'ge Miles per Hour.
			Miles.	No. Hours	
St. Louis, Mo., & Memphis, Tenn. }	Every Monday & Thursday.	8.00 A.M			
P. R. R. Terminus, "	" Monday & Thursday.	6.00 P.M	160	10	16
Springfield, "	" Wednesday & Saturday	7.45 A.M	143	37¾	3½
Fayetteville, "	" Thursday & Sunday,	10.15 A.M	100	26½	3½
Fort Smith, Ark.	" Friday & Monday,	3.30 A.M	65	17¼	3½
Sherman, Texas	" Sunday & Wednesday,	12.30 A.M	205	45	4½
Fort Belknap. "	" Monday & Thursday,	9.00 A.M	146½	32½	4½
Fort Chadbourn, "	" Tuesday & Friday,	3.15 P.M	136	30¼	4½
Pecos River, (Em. Crossing.)	" Thursday & Sunday,	3.45 A.M	165	36½	4½
El Paso,	" Saturday & Tuesday,	11.00 A.M	248½	55½	4½
Soldier's Farewell	" Sunday & Wednesday,	8.30 P.M	150	33½	4½
Tucson, Arizona	" Tuesday & Friday,	1.30 P.M	184½	41	4½
Gila River,* "	" Wednesday & Saturday	9.00 P.M	141	31½	4½
Fort Yuma, Cal.	" Friday & Monday,	3.00 A.M	135	30	4½
San Bernardino "	" Saturday & Tuesday,	11.00 P.M	200	44	4½
Ft. Tejon, (Via Los Angeles)	" Monday & Thursday,	7.30 A.M	150	32½	4½
Visalia, "	" Tuesday & Friday,	11.30 A.M	127	28	4½
Firebaugh's Ferry, "	" Wednesday & Saturday	5.30 A.M	82	18	4½
(Arrive) San Francisco,	" Thursday & Sunday,	8.30 A.M	163	27	6

GOING EAST.

LEAVE.	DAYS.	Hour.	Distance, Place to Place.	Time allowed.	Av'ge Miles per Hour.
			Miles.	No. Hours	
San Francisco, Cal.	Every Monday & Thursday,	8.00 A.M			
Firebaugh's Ferry, "	" Tuesday & Friday,	11.00 A.M	163	27	6
Visalia, "	" Wednesday & Saturday,	5.00 A.M	82	18	4½
Ft. Tejon, (Via Los Angeles)	" Thursday & Sunday,	9.00 A.M	127	28	4½
San Bernardino, "	" Friday & Monday,	5.30 P.M	150	32½	4½
Fort Yuma, "	" Sunday & Wednesday,	1.30 P.M	200	44	4½
Gila River,* Arizona	" Monday & Thursday,	7.30 P.M	135	30	4½
Tucson, "	" Wednesday & Saturday	3.00 A.M	141	31½	4½
Soldier's Farewell,	" Thursday & Sunday,	8.00 P.M	184½	41	4½
El Paso, Tex.	" Saturday & Tuesday,	5.30 A.M	150	33½	4½
Pecos River, (Em. Crossing.)	" Monday & Thursday	12.45 P.M	248½	55½	4½
Fort Chadbourn, "	" Wednesday & Saturday	1.15 A.M	165	36½	4½
Fort Belknap, "	" Thursday & Sunday,	7.30 A.M	136	30¼	4½
Sherman, "	" Friday & Monday,	4.00 P.M	146½	32½	4½
Fort Smith, Ark.	" Sunday & Wednesday,	1.00 P.M	205	45	4½
Fayetteville, Mo.	" Monday, & Thursday,	6.15 A.M	65	17¼	3½
Springfield, "	" Tuesday & Friday,	8.45 A.M	100	26½	3½
P. R. R. Terminus, "	" Wednesday & Saturday	10.30 P.M	143	37¾	3½
(Arrive) St. Louis, Mo., & Memphis, Tenn. }	" Thursday & Sunday,		160	10	16

This Schedule may not be exact—Superintendents, Agents, Station-men, Conductors, Drivers and all employees are particularly directed to use every possible exertion to get the Stages through in quick time, even though they may be ahead of this time.

If they are behind this time, it will be necessary to urge the animals on to the highest speed that they can be driven without injury.

Remember that no allowance is made in the time for ferries, changing teams, &c. It is therefore necessary that each driver increase his speed over the average per hour enough to gain the necessary time for meals, changing teams, crossing ferries, &c.

Every person in the Company's employ will always bear in mind that each minute of time is of importance. If each driver on the route loses fifteen (15) minutes, it would make a total loss of time, on the entire route, of twenty-five (25) hours, or, more than one day. If each one loses ten (10) minutes it would make a total loss of sixteen and one half (16½) hours, or, the best part of a day.

On the contrary, if each driver gains that amount of time, it leaves a margin of time against accidents and extra delays.

All hands will see the great necessity of promptness and dispatch: every minute of time is valuable as the Company are under heavy forfeit if the mail is behind time.

Conductors must note the hour and date of departure from Stations, the causes of delay, if any, and all particulars. They must also report the same fully to their respective Superintendents.

* The Station referred to on Gila River, is 40 miles west of Maricopa Wells.

JOHN BUTTERFIELD.
Pres't.

Butterfield Overland Mail Company Schedule

Fig: 5[99]

FORT CHADBOURNE,TEXAS

Charles Schuchard Lithograph
Fort Chadbourne 1856

Fig: 6

Chapter XIX

Samuel Maverick

Samuel Augustus Maverick was an entrepreneur of the 1800's. He had foresight to see buying land as an investment, and buy land he did. In the 1840's Maverick owned over thirty-five thousand acres of land in Bexar County alone, and had as much by survey.

Sam was a lawyer, served in the Texas Legislature, and the term "maverick" stems from his name. Many believe Samuel Maverick was not only a land baron, but a cattle baron too. The latter though was not necessarily the truth. As it was told, Sam never owned over four hundred head of cattle. He received those in lieu of a twelve hundred dollar debt, owed him from an individual that could not repay him in cash. Sam, not really being interested in cattle, never bothered to brand them, so when his cattle mixed with other rancher's cows, they used the term, "that's one of Mavericks". The word progressed, and found its way into the dictionary apparently for the first time in 1867. In the current Webster's the definition is: mav-er-ick, n. [after S. Maverick (1803-70), Texas rancher who did not brand his cattle] 1. an unbranded animal, 2. a person who takes an independent stand.

Through the years, he continued to buy land in Texas, and that is the reason Samuel Maverick becomes part of the history of Fort Chadbourne. On March 27, 1853, he had surveyed a portion of the land that included Fort Chadbourne. Survey No. 301, Section 9, situated on Oak Creek, a branch of the Colorado River. Chain carriers for the project were Jose Mercedes and Jesus Garza. A year later on March 10, 1854, survey No. 301, along with No. 300, were patented to Samuel A. Maverick assignee, and were the locations of present day Fort Chadbourne.

This patent would later lead Mr. Maverick to charge the United States Government for the occupancy of his land and resources. As early as 1853, a year earlier than the actual patent was assigned, and three years before the agreement was reached, military correspondence from Lt. Colonel Washington Seawell at Fort Chadbourne, made mention of the post being situated on land leased from Mr. Maverick of San Antonio. Also interesting to note was the agreement. When reached, it dated back to November 1, 1852, when allocating rent was first due, long before Mr. Maverick actually owned the property. But, it wasn't until September 29, 1856, that an article of agreement was actually made and entered into between Lt. Colonel A. C. Myers, U. S. Army, Assistant Quartermaster, Department of Texas, on the one part, and Samuel Augustus Maverick, of Bexar County, Texas, of the other part. Maverick agreed that he, his heirs, executors and administrators, "shall let, rent and lease to the United States of America a certain tract and parcel of Land, lying and being situated in the County of Bexar and State of Texas, and described as follows: All that tract of Land, which has been and is now occupied as a Military Post, and known as Fort Chadbourne, situated on Oak Creek a branch of the Red Fork of the Colorado River, said Land being known as Survey No. 301 in Section No. 9, and contains three hundred and twenty acres... The said tract of Land being granted to the said Samuel A. Maverick as assignee of James Gross, by the State of

Texas, as is shown by Letter Patent No. 43 in Vol. No. 10.

"The United States or their Officers and Agents are to hold the said premises with rights and appurtenances thereto belongs, so long as they or any portion of them may be required by the United States for occupancy as a Military Post, not however to exceed the period of Twenty years, dating from the first day of November one thousand eight hundred and fifty two, reserving the privilege to the United States, to cut and use any timber or other material which maybe found upon the land herein before described and which may be required for the erection or repairs of any and all public buildings and fences, or for other purposes connected with the Military Post of Fort Chadbourne. Also, the right to cut and use from the described Survey of Land whatever wood may be required for fuel for the use of troops which now or may hereafter occupy the said Military Post of Fort Chadbourne; For and in consideration of which the United States are to pay to the said Samuel A. Maverick, his heirs, executors or administrators the sum of twenty five dollars per month rent, for the premises and privileges granted by this lease, from and after the first day of November one thousand eight hundred and fifty two, being the date of the first occupancy of the said Post. It is further agreed on the part of the United States, that the buildings, fences, erections and improvements now made and which may be hereafter made on the aforesaid described survey, shall be left thereon for the benefit of the said Samuel A. Maverick, when they shall no longer be required by the United States.

"If the United States shall at any period before the termination of this Lease wish to purchase the aforesaid described Survey of Land and premises, the said Samuel A. Maverick his heirs, executors and administrators binds himself to sell the same to the United States at ($10.00) Ten Dollars per acre if purchases by the First day of January One thousand Eight hundred and Sixty, or at ($20.00) Twenty Dollars per acre if purchases by the First day of January One thousand Eight hundred and Sixty, or at ($20.00) Twenty Dollars per acre if purchased after that date, and make a transfer by a good and sufficient title in the form required by Law.

"And the said Samuel A. Maverick his heirs, executors and administrators further agrees and contracts to guaranty and defend the United States against all claims of whatsoever nature for rents or damages for or on account of the use and occupancy of the said tract of Land and premises, and for all wood, hay, posts, timbers or anything else which may have been cut or taken from any Lands contained in the said tract or Survey from the date of the first occupancy of the Land hereinbefore described and belonging to the said Samuel A. Maverick."

The contract was accompanied by a cover letter dated September 27, 1856, and written by A. C. Myers, Bvt. Lt. Colonel A. Q. M., Office A.Q.M. Department of Texas, San Antonio, to Major General Thomas S. Jesup, Q. M. General U.S.A., Washington City, D.C.: "I have the honor to transmit herewith, two copies approved by the Colonel commanding the Department of Texas, of a lease for the present site of Fort Chadbourne, Texas.

"The lease with Mr. Maverick includes the Fort, made with Messrs. Howard and Twohig on the 12th February 1855, and approved by General Persifor F. Smith, then commanding the Department of Texas, includes the wood tract adjacent to Fort Chadbourne."[100]

In May, a few months before the contract was signed, Maverick was at Fort Chadbourne to pick up a pack of mules for a survey along the Red Fork of the Colorado, which followed the emigrant trail established by Randolph Marcy in 1849. In writing to his wife Mary, he exuberated good health, while describing the beauty of Chadbourne. He referred to the nights as a "little bit frosty" for that time of year.[101]

It wasn't until September 12, 1857, that Samuel Maverick received some reimbursement for back rent from the U. S. Treasury. War draft on New Orleans, No. 3557, for nine hundred fifty dollars was issued to him. Mr. Maverick did not agree with the amount, explaining the lease stipulated he was to be paid from November 1, 1852. The check he received would cover up to January 1, 1856, but it was now September 1857, so he noted rent for that time was still due. Maverick figured it up to the exact day adding, as of this day, September 20, 1857 this equals eight months and twenty days, at twenty-five dollars per month. Figuring the months, January through August, plus twenty days in September, the total balance due Maverick at that time was two hundred sixteen dollars and sixty-seven cents. Maverick was definitely a business man!

In September of 1861, Maverick's son, Samuel Maverick, Jr., was stationed at Fort Chadbourne and listed as a Private serving in Company B of McCulloch's Texas Mounted Riflemen. On the regimental return he was listed as sick since the nineteenth of August.

Maverick's other son, Lewis Maverick, was a Captain in Company E of the 36th Texas Cavalry of Woods Regiment, stationed in San Antonio. He enlisted Private George M. Maverick, his brother, age seventeen, on March 29, 1862, in San Antonio, Texas for three years.

In January 1862, correspondence to Major Samuel Boyer Davis from Henry McCulloch, suggested that Private Samuel Maverick, Jr., along with two other young men from Company B 1st Regiment of the Texas Mounted Rifleman be allowed furlough prior to the first of February. McCulloch bragged on these clean young men who were fine soldiers, and stated they would make very good officers.

Samuel A. Maverick owned the Fort Chadbourne property until his death on September 2, 1870, at which time fifty per cent of his holdings went to his wife Mary, and the other fifty per cent to his children. In January 1876, the children transferred all the land of the James Gross Survey, which included Survey No. 301, Section 9, to their mother Mary. On October 24, 1877, Mary A. Maverick sold three hundred and twenty acres of land, which included historic Fort Chadbourne, to Lucinda S. Odom, wife of Thomas L. Odom for five hundred dollars in gold.

On that day a new legacy would begin for this old Fort. Although the family had already owned other land in the area since 1874, the addition of the Fort Chadbourne property in 1877 would become the heart of the family. Thomas and Lucinda Odom would use its buildings as headquarters, barns, and bunk houses to build one of the largest ranches in West Texas. Through the years, eight generations of grandchildren would play "Cowboys and Indians" within its historic walls, and a family heritage like few others would be built.

Fort Chadbourne
The Family Heritage

Old Fort Chadbourne

Chapter XX

Thomas Lawson Odom

Thomas Lawson Odom was born March 20, 1825, in Conecuh County, Alabama. His first wife, Lucinda S. Milstead was born March 21, 1829, also in Alabama. They were married in Escambia, Florida on October 28, 1845, and some records suggest a move was made to Texas in 1853. Census showed the fourth child Sedonia was born in April 1854 in Birmingham, Alabama. An exact date was impossible, although Thomas may have arrived in late 1853, leaving his pregnant wife to deliver in Alabama before making the trip to Texas. All together they had thirteen children; Sarah Frances, Ancelia, Garland Good, Sedonia K., John Patrick, Stephen A. Douglas, George Washington, Cyrus Wallace, Lula M., Nelly, Thomas Lawson, Jr., John M., and William Edgar Odom.

The family settled in the San Antonio area. They owned and operated a saw mill, and were in the shingle making business during the 1850's when many of the frontier forts were being built. It is quite possible that some of their cypress shingles were actually used on the buildings located at Fort Chadbourne. It is also a plausible scenario that when Thomas Odom was delivering these shingles, he first laid eyes on this area of Texas, and began to consider buying land here. At that time, little did he know, one day he and his family would call Fort Chadbourne home.

Thomas Odom served as a private in the Confederate States Army during the Civil War. He was enlisted into Captain J. O. Adams' Company of Texas Cavalry, guarding the Commissary at San Antonio, Texas. He served on detached duty, mainly in the Fredericksburg area, for the remainder of the war and at its close Odom was discharged in San Antonio.

Colonel Odom, as he was respectfully called throughout his entire life, made his first land purchases in Bexar County in 1856. Followed by property in Medina County in 1865 post Civil War, and again in 1871, when his first collaboration with the Maverick family took place.

The following years, prior to his purchase of Fort Chadbourne in 1877, he and his son Garland drove cattle from San Antonio to Kansas. In 1876 they established the O D Ranch, when they drove thirty-six thousand head of cattle into the vicinity of Fort Chadbourne. The next year, with the purchase of the Fort property, it would become the headquarters of this newly established cattle ranch. [102]

From that point, land acquisition was slow, but steady, as more land was purchased around the Fort Chadbourne property, including land in today's Taylor, Nolan, Coke, Tom Green, and Runnels counties. Much of the property purchased skirted Oak Creek, and by 1883, the Odom's had acquired approximately forty-two thousand acres of land. Survey 309, northwest of the Fort, was purchased from cattlemen James E. McCord and E. A. Lindsey, of Runnels County, along with property from the estate of Richard Howard, who was a strong competitor to Samuel Maverick in amassing considerable property throughout West Texas during the 1850's. Besides the land abutting Oak Creek in Coke County, much of the other acreage was purchased in and around the Fish and Valley Creek vicinities in Runnels and Taylor counties. It was the same then as it is today; access to water was one of the most pivotal requirements when the Odom's made their decision for acquiring land.

During this time Thomas Odom was elected as County Commissioner, and later he served the great State of Texas as its delegate. That occurred on November 7, 1882 when he was elected to the Texas 78th District House of Representatives.

1884 would be a year to test Odom's patience both in the Texas Legislature, and at home on his land. On January 7, 1884, Odom used his influence with Governor John Ireland[103] to call a special session, to pass a law making fence cutting a felony. In his speech to the House, he stressed that the legislature had favored the fence cutters, and was trying to crush out of existence the greatest enterprise in Texas, cattle ranching. As it was, these ragtag and bobtail ruffians had cost the people of the State of Texas more than ten thousand dollars in damages.

In his tirade during the session, Odom stated he was ready to fight to keep Texas one and inseparable, but if justice was not done to all classes, both cattlemen and fence cutters, he would be glad to see the state divided and would vote for it.

This amounted to a war between large land owners, and poor squatters of cattlemen, who had operated on others open range for years. Then a thing called barb wire made its debut, and the wide open spaces of Texas soon became a thing of the past. Men such as Thomas Odom owned huge spreads, covering some ninety thousand acres of land. As he, and other land owners like him, began to fence their properties, the squatters who had allowed their cattle to roam free, and graze off these open spaces, were slowly being driven off. This left them no way to feed their cattle, which in turn proved hard for them to provide for their families. This caused the downtrodden individuals to revolt against those whose land they had trespassed on for years. They now called these land owners the enemy, simply because these men of wealth, had decided to fence what they had bought and paid for, and use for their own purpose.

Soon a gang, right in Odom's backyard was formed, and they began their nightly raids against Odom, and the barb wire. Miles of barb wire were cut by these men, while leaving their nightly calling card pinned to the fence as a "notice" to their intentions, not to allow any peace to follow.

In the following months, T. L. Odom used his contacts, such as Governor Ireland, to inform him of these ongoing problems, and that if left unchecked things would only get worse.

By this time the cocky fence cutters had cut and destroyed approximately four miles of his fence. Odom expected Governor Ireland to step up, and send an experienced and expert detective in order to catch the culprits behind these continued schemes on his and his neighbor's fences. Odom was also willing to foot much of the bill, as long as the offenders were caught and convicted. He suggested to Ireland, that they infiltrate the group with a young man who could be a part of the fence cutters gang, and learn their wicked ways. If something was not done soon, there would be greater losses to bear. In January 1884, Governor Ireland convinced the Texas Legislature to appropriate fifty thousand dollars for rewards and undercover work.[104]

In the meantime, a couple of months later, seven more miles of Odom's fence was cut. In the Austin Daily Statesman, April 19, 1884, an article appeared concerning the ongoing mischief these men continued to impose on the ranchers and the men and families who worked for them. One night after destroying more of Odom's fence, the men pulled up a post located near Odom's home, and swung it up in a tree. An attached note read, "Here you hang. If you don't stop building this pasture you'll find yourself shot like this post. We don't intend that any pasture fence shall stand in this country. We mean business." This group known as the Fish Creek Fence Cutters Gang, and a young man by the name of Benjamin Goodin Warren, unbeknownst to the gang, was about to make their acquaintance. Soon he was sworn in to become a member of this despicable bunch of men. At the same time, Benjamin Goodin Warren was also sworn in to Captain J. T. Gillespie's Company E, as a Private in the Frontier Battalion of the Texas Rangers. His undercover work had begun.

On May 4, 1884, the Texas Rangers made arrest on eight men, and charged them with fence cutting. A total of fifteen men were indicted in Runnels County alone, based upon the work of Texas Ranger Warren. This placed Warren in a precarious situation. Until these men were tried and put away, they intended revenge in the worst way, and meant to put a stop to Benjamin Warren from ever testifying at a trial against them.

In February 1885, the trial was to begin against the men Ben Warren had named, and who were indicted by a grand jury in May of 1884.

On the night of February 10, 1885, Ranger Ben Warren and Thomas Odom were in Nolan County, Sweetwater, Texas, to testify the next day against the gang members. Odom and Warren were sitting with others next to a stove in the office of the Central Hotel; Warren sat in a chair, his hands in his pockets, while smoking a pipe. From outside a window, someone fired a gun, and the bullet passed by Odom's head before it struck Warren in the face under the left eye, then exited behind the right ear, and lodged in the wall beyond. It killed him instantly. Warren never moved nor spoke, while blood bubbled from the wound under his eye.

Many of the Fish Creek Gang was seen at a saloon near the Central Hotel in Sweetwater, Texas that night. On June 25, 1885, brothers Neil Boyett and C. W. Boyett, along with W. J. "Bud" Wood were arrested. All three were men Warren was to testify against.

Odom later testified that he, and Ben Warren, were sitting around the stove with other men, when the sudden crack of a gunshot rang out. He said he sprang from his chair, and passed rapidly into the adjoining dining room, thinking that he had been fired upon. On turning in the dining room, and looking back into the office, he saw blood spurting from Warren's face. Odom called for someone to prevent Warren's body from falling, and to get a doctor. Odom in fear of his own life, then closed the dining room door, and remained there a few minutes in the dark. About that time, Odom thought he saw the flash of light on the window panes, north of where he stood, and presently a gentleman entered the dining room from the adjoining room. Odom told him Ben Warren had been shot. After a few minutes Odom walked out of the dining room, through the kitchen, and went to the Palace Hotel, where he secured his quarters and retired for the night.

The next morning he saw the dead body of Benjamin Warren still in the office of the Central Hotel. The ball had passed into the head, just below the right ear. It entered the room, from the west side of the third window on the north side, counting from the northeast corner of the building. The stove sat about ten feet from the window, through which the ball entered the room. That window was at an angle of about fifty or sixty degrees towards the front of the building. Odom had been sitting about three feet south of the stove, and nearly on a line between the front and dining room doors. When the shot was fired, he was in the act of punching the fire with his head inclined slightly forward. Warren was sitting about four feet to the right of Odom.

Odom examined the bullet hole in the window the next morning. He also examined the grounds outside, and found a track of a man, the toe of the right foot showing very plainly against the bottom plank of the fence. Odom had handled firearms since he was ten years old, and it was his opinion that if shot from this track, the fatal ball must have been fired by someone shooting from the left shoulder.[105]

On February 17, 1885, Thomas Odom brought Ben Warren's body back to Fort Chadbourne to be laid to rest next to his brother who had passed away in infancy. His grave stone still standing today reads:

"Farewell my wife and children all. From you a father Christ doth call." He was survived by his wife Eppie Hubbert Warren and ten children, one of whom was born eight months after his murder. He served less than one year as a Texas Ranger.

The three men indicted of Warren's murder were tried under several changes of venue. W. J. Wood was tried in Callahan County, convicted and sentenced to life in prison for first degree murder. He appealed, and his case was reversed because the sheriff, coroner, and county attorney held him as a material witness while he was a suspect, and had him testify at the Coroner's inquest without advising him of his rights.

C. W. Boyett was tried in Taylor County, and convicted and sentenced to life in prison for the first degree murder. He appealed, but the appeals court affirmed the conviction.

No record has been located that shows Neil Boyett was ever tried. W. J. Wood was never retried, and C. W. Boyett although convicted, no record shows where he served time for the offense.

The author diligently searched the Texas Convict Records Ledger for the years around the 1885 time period, but was unable to locate the names of any of the men associated with the murder of Ben Warren, including that of C. W. Boyett who was sentenced to life in prison.

A grave of a C. W. Boyett, at Hilton Cemetery, in Nolan County, the area Boyett lived in at the time of the murder, and the county where the murder of Ben Warren took place was located. Date of death on the tombstone, December 1900, some fifteen years after the murder of Texas Ranger Warren.   Assumption would lead us to believe this was the same man, but at this time, and without further details, there is no way of knowing one hundred per cent. But, odds are he is one and the same.

Ben Warren
Texas Ranger
B: 01-27-1843   D: 02-10-1885

Chapter XXI

Ranching

Although ranchers eventually won their battles with fence cutters, it also presented them with other problems intermittently rancher to rancher.   In May 1886, such a problem arose when a trail drive under the Odom Luckett Land and Cattle Company brand was halted at a guarded gate on the Spur Ranch, in Garza County.

The Odom Luckett Land and Cattle Company was established in 1879, as a partnership between Garland Odom, oldest son of Thomas Odom, and brother-in-law Henry H. Luckett, who was married to Garland's sister Sedonia.   In the years that followed, the cattle company drove thousands of head of cattle north to Kansas. Much property was derived from other family member's interest being consolidated into the company, who sold their inheritance from their

Mother's estate. By 1894, when the original charter lapsed, the two men owned all the capital stock, and at that time a decision was made to dissolve the company. Garland Odom took the west half retaining Fort Chadbourne as his ranching headquarters.

During this time just as Thomas and Garland Odom had begun to fence their land, the large ranches in north Texas such as Charlie Goodnight's JA Ranch, and the Spur Ranch, in Garza County did the same. Eventually this served two purposes. First and foremost the original purpose was to keep trespassers off their land, but when the Texas Fever became an enormous problem for the ranchers in southern Texas, the northern cattle ranchers used these fenced areas to guard against the risk of contamination to their own livestock.

Rather than go into great detail on the history of what has been nicknamed the "Winchester Quarantine", because when necessary many of the men used Winchester rifles to enforce their point, it is simply touched upon because of the event surrounding the occurrence that took place in 1886.

It wasn't until 1893 when "Texas Fever" was rectified, and found to be carried by cattle ticks. After sucking blood from an infected cow, and falling to the ground, the ticks laid eggs which when hatched were already contaminated with the disease, and infected the pastures along the way. The land owners in those areas, in order to protect their own investments, had no choice but to do whatever possible to stop the spread of the disease by halting the cattle drives from crossing their land. They lobbied to have ranchers from South Texas use a special trail set aside for passage. Of course, many times these regulations were tested, and so it was on that day in May 1886, when the Odom trail boss demanded entry through the Spur Ranch claiming the gate was blocking an official road.[106]

In the meantime, owners of the Spur Ranch stood tall in the saddle and sent for a ruling while armed guards protected their range and refused to let the cattle drive pass through their fenced property. A rider from the ranch was sent to Snyder, in Scurry County, for an assessment, which was upheld in the Spur Ranch's favor. Upon learning of the legal decision, the Odom Luckett drovers had no choice but to skirt the ranchland, and comply by using another route.

In all actuality this time period was the beginning of the end for large cattle drives heading to Kansas. Men such as Odom began to find newer and better ways to send their cattle north, bypassing the many problems they faced on long cattle drives. It was known as the railroad.

Besides fence cutting, drought, and disease on the frontier, there was always the threat of Indian Depredations. One such problem was so prevalent for years, with the raiding of horses and livestock, that the ranchers filed for restitution to recoup some of their losses. In a court document, dated January 2, 1894, the Court of Claims of the United States, Indian Depredations, No. 9202, in the transcript of Thomas L. Odom vs. The United States, Mr. Odom's deposition related that every year from 1865 through 1873, that he had lost horses and mules to the Comanche Indians. He placed a total value of loss at $6,770.00. Judgments were not rendered in favor of claimants for these Indian Depredations until some ten years later, and many years after Thomas Odom had died. Final judgment, Case Number 390, May 21, 1914, Runnels County, Texas, was in the amount of $960.00, much less than the original claim. It was paid and divided amongst the descendents of Thomas Odom.

Thomas Lawson Odom led a very eventful and productive life. His heritage still lives through his family and Fort Chadbourne. We will never know how Fort Chadbourne would have been remembered if Thomas and Lucinda had not purchased those first 320 acres of land that contained this frontier post, or passed on its enduring legacy to their family for many generations to come.

Lucinda S. Milstead Odom passed away on August 21, 1882. Thomas Odom remarried in 1884, to Mary Hunt McCaleb, originally from Vicksburg, Mississippi, and later of Galveston, Texas. Mary was a prolific poet. She and Thomas met through correspondence about her poems, and soon married. Following the marriage, her husband published a book of her life's work in poetry, which included a dedication and poem to her beloved. The dedication read:

"To the best and dearest friend I have on Earth

My Husband

Hon. T. L. Odom

Of Fort Chadbourne, Runnels County, Texas

With the deepest affection of his devoted wife
The Author"

Thomas Lawson Odom passed away on March 29, 1897 at age 72. He was buried at Fort Chadbourne Cemetery next to his first wife Lucinda. Mary Hunt McCaleb Odom died August 6, 1925 at age 85, and was buried in Oakwood Cemetery, Austin, Texas.

Thomas Lawson Odom

03-20-1825   **03-29-1897**

Garland Good and Sallie Crigler Odom

Son and daughter-in-law of Thomas Odom

Conda Holt Wylie

12-07-1882   01-06-1969

Conda Odom Richards

B: 5-13-1926

Utica, New York

D: 8-19-1998

Buried:

Fort Chadbourne

Cemetery

Nell Papasan Richards

B: 12-10-1929

Lawn, Texas

Garland and Lana Richards

Chapter XXII

Conda Wylie

Garland Odom, oldest son of Thomas and Lucinda, married Miss Sallie M. Crigler, daughter of Honorable Judge Ruben and Eleanor Crigler, in San Antonio, Texas, on January 28, 1875. The marriage produced two daughters; Lou Nettie and Edna M. Odom. It is apparent ranching was deep seeded in the Odom genes. Garland Odom always held the same interest in cattle ranching as his father, and after he established the O D Ranch with him, he remained at its helm long after Thomas Odom passed away.

For many years, Garland and Sallie Odom resided in what today is presented as the Double Officers Quarters, and early Ranching Headquarters. That building burned in September 1919. After the fire they moved to Ballinger, Texas in Runnels County, but Odom continued to head the ranch.

Besides cattle ranching, Odom was a very astute businessman. In 1909, Odom along with a group of his associates, including a brother-in-law, formed the Farmers and Merchants Bank in Ballinger. Odom also owned several buildings as well as the Central Hotel, the largest three story hotel in Ballinger at the time. It was constructed for a cost of eighty-five thousand dollars.

Their daughter Edna was born at Fort Chadbourne on September 17, 1884, and later married Conda Holt Wylie on December 14, 1904. Census showed they resided with the Odom's in the early years of marriage, but later moved to Fort Chadbourne into a small house located on the ranch. Through the years the house was enlarged on several different occasions, including a new kitchen and dining room added in 1938, and major remodeling was done in 1954, which made it a grand showplace for its generation.

I grew up in the area, and was always aware of Conda Wylie. Although Mr. Wylie was a very generous man, his view of Fort Chadbourne was much different from that of his great grandson today. He believed Fort Chadbourne to be a working cattle ranch, and utilized the buildings as barns and storage. He did not relish the idea of weekend historians wanting to freely roam the grounds of his ranch, searching for artifacts of times past. Too many times his saddles, his tools, his personal possessions walked off the premises. So for Mr. Wylie, the easiest way to protect what was rightfully his was to keep these trespassers at bay. It is not far fetched to say Mr. Wylie did not mind escorting these intruders from his property, while accompanied by his trusty Colt 45.

Although some of those that made contact with Mr. Wylie on one of those adventures might not praise him for his generous soul, there is too many worthwhile accomplishments to list that the Wylie's graciously did for the area that far outweigh his occasional ornery nature. In 1955, along with their sister-in-law Nettie Currie, the Wylie's funded the building of a new Methodist Church in Ballinger. Their resources established the Jay Rollins Library at McMurry College, but one of Conda and Edna Wylie's most enduring legacies was their kinship with the West Texas Rehabilitation Center in Abilene, Texas. In 1960, West Texas Rehabilitation Center's Executive Director, Shelley Smith, came to Mr. Wylie one day and asked for a donation to help the center. Mr. Wylie always willing to help those who helped themselves, or those less fortunate, was quick to answer "I'd like too, but." He explained that rancher's cash flow was not always steady. There were good years and bad years, rainy years and drought. He added, sometimes a man can be wealthy in "heads of cattle", but still strapped for cash.

So, Mr. Wylie offered Shelley Smith an alternative to a cash donation. He offered to give him twenty calves, and conveyed to him that he felt sure other ranchers would be willing to do the same. Rehab could then auction the cattle and retain any and all proceeds generated by the sale. Shelley Smith not willing to turn down any opportunity quickly accepted Mr. Wylie's brainstorm and the rest is now history.

That was the beginning of one of the Rehabs most lucrative proposals, and they are still quick to give Mr. Wylie credit for this momentous idea. In its beginning the cattle sale was called "Round Up for Crippled Children." Today it is simply called Round up for Rehab! To date those auctions have raised over eleven million dollars for the West Texas Rehabilitation Center.

In continuing the legacy, Mr. Wylie's great grandson Garland Richards was honored in 2009 with The Good Neighbor Harry Holt Award. It is given for exemplary dedication, support, and promotion of the West Texas Rehabilitation Center.

The Wylie's daughter Maurine and son-in-law Edmund showed little interest in the ranch. They had two sons, Edmund "Bud" Richards, and Conda Odom Richards. Their second son and Mr. Wylie's namesake Conda was so taken with ranching that he came to live with his grandfather at an early age. Following his service in the Navy during World War II, where he was a machinist, he returned to Fort Chadbourne to follow in his grandfather's footsteps. Mr. Wylie died on January 6, 1969, and the ranch was left to his grandson Conda Richards. Conda operated the ranch with the love of his life Nell Papasan Richards, and their three children Brian, Garland, and Sallie.

Besides ranching, the Odom's, Wylie's, and Richards' also had an interest in banking. Conda Richards, just as his great grandfather Garland Odom, and Grandfather Conda Wylie had done, added banking to his resume. In the mid nineteen fifties Mr. Wylie owned one-third interest in the First National Bank of Ballinger, while also serving as a Board of Director. In 1966, grandson Conda Richards purchased his grandfathers interest along with that of Mr. F. M. Pearce, and Mr. Ralph Erwin, to gain controlling interest in the bank. After twenty years as Chairman of Board and CEO, a heart attack alerted Conda Richards to slow down, and his oldest son, Brian Richards became Chief Operating Officer.

In 1998 Conda Richards died of a heart attack, and the ranch was apportioned out to his three children. The only remaining original ranch property still in family hands today belongs to Garland Richards, and his wife Lana, which also includes Historic Fort Chadbourne.

Fort Chadbourne
The Reconstruction

Chapter XXIII

Form a Foundation

Reconstruct a Fort

On several occasions I have heard Garland Richards relate a story concerning driving into the Fort one morning after a rain. As he passed one of the buildings, a section of its side crumbled to the ground. He said at that time, I stopped and said to myself, "That will be the last rock I watch fall."

Many times I have referred to Garland as stubborn. Yes, even in his presence, but I do it as a respect for who he is, because it is his stubbornness that made him succeed. He and his wife Lana began a task that at the time, even they had no idea could possibly turn into a full time, life altering project. Restoring a historic old Fort was a major undertaking. Who would ever dream of doing such a thing?

Not having a clue what it entailed, or the demands it would place on them never seemed to bother either of them. Besides the property encompassing Fort Chadbourne, Garland had been left a small monetary inheritance when his father died, and he and Lana decided to use a portion of that money to begin the formation of the foundation. They rolled up their sleeves and dug in. Numerous times they were told it could not be done, and at times they wondered the same thing, but they never gave up. Even when a historical architect conveyed to them that the buildings, especially the enlisted men's barracks, could not be reconstructed in its present dilapidated state; "you need to give up, tear it down and rebuild" he told them, they did not give up or give in. To Garland this was nothing more than a challenge and he refused to tear down a structure that had stood on his land since 1852. Out of remembrance of the soldiers and teamsters who had painstakingly quarried and laid each stone, he was determined to at least attempt the reconstruction without total demolition of these buildings. So the architect finally threw up his hands and said, "show me", and show him he did.

In 2003, Garland was presented with the Preservation Texas Award for his ingenious idea and work. Garland in his presentations today always makes note, "I'm a rancher, and ranchers rebuild, patch it up, and make it last another year." So he did what he and other ranchers do best, figure out a way and get to work on it. Sometimes it works, sometimes it doesn't, but this time ended with great success.

It took six months of preparation just to get ready for a job that would take but a few hours to complete on each wall. In order to support and align the dilapidated rock walls, braces and turnbuckles were used to guide the crooked walls back into place. Once the walls were horizontally and vertically leveled, an air bladder pump was employed to pressure the grout in between each rock for added strength and stabilization.

An analysis was done by Joe Freeman, Historical Architect from Austin, Texas on the aged mortar to find the percentage of sand and cement used in the 1850's. In the final process, additional white portland cement was added to make the mixture stronger, and surprisingly more resistant to rodents. Rodents had a tendency to scratch out the old grout and house into the mortar, so the decision was made in order to ensure longer preservation, to make the new mixture a harder, more substantial substance thus obliterating the rodent problem in the future. This procedure was used throughout the Fort on all ruins and newly restored buildings.

Today as you tour Fort Chadbourne you will see a great progress that no one could have foreseen. Hours, days, months, years have passed since February 1, 1999, when the Foundation Certificate of Incorporation became effective, but when you look at it from rubble to restoration, it is simply amazing what transpired in those ten years.

With the aid of the first contribution of $374,000.00 in 2001 from the Dodge Jones Foundation in Abilene, Texas, work began and has never slowed down.

Six historic buildings, including the Single Officers Quarter's, Double Officers Quarter's, Enlisted Men's Barracks, Root Cellar, and Butterfield Stage Stop have been reconstructed and brought back to life. In fact, at this time, the Butterfield Stage Station is the only restored Butterfield Stage Stop in the State of Texas. All other ruins including the Hospital and

Commanding Officer's Quarters have been fully stabilized.

With the aid of Larry Riemenschneider, an archeological steward with the Texas Historical Commission and the Concho Valley Archeological Society, archeological investigations were completed on all the buildings before restoration could take place. Over five hundred thousand artifacts have been cataloged to date. These excavations are still ongoing in some areas, and publications of all archeological findings on each restored structure are available.

Fort Chadbourne was very lucky to find such wonderful and hard working volunteers, as the ones connected with the CVAS. But, one other group calling themselves the SMARTS (Special Military Active Retired Travel Club) has been very consequential. These men and women who served our country proud, "adopted" Fort Chadbourne several years ago, and volunteer at least two weeks a year, to do anything and everything to benefit the Fort. Many of them also volunteer at other events held throughout the year at Fort Chadbourne. Without them several projects, such as excavations, painting, and woodworking would have taken much longer to complete.

The Fort Chadbourne Cavalry and Artillery groups, who represent Fort Chadbourne around the state, and participate in all Fort Chadbourne events, have logged over 10,000 hours of volunteer work. They make the fort come alive with realistic reenactments, and are greatly appreciated for their representation of Fort Chadbourne.

One cannot mention artifacts at Fort Chadbourne without referring to W. T. (Dub) Davis, or Dewey Chesnut; two gentlemen who had previously worked on the ranch while employed with then, Humble Oil Company. Once the decision was made to form the Foundation, and to open the Fort to the public, many significant artifacts still laid atop the ground. These two men were delighted to be asked to freely roam these grounds, and discover many of the treasures now on display at Fort Chadbourne. All items located were mapped and cataloged as to location, and identified whenever possible.

Dub was also a witcher, or dowser if you prefer, and visited several times a month before moving to be closer to his children. Always carried in his hand was his "witching stick", commonly known as a divining rod. Dub spent hours wandering the grounds, and fascinated everyone he met with his many discoveries, and his exciting anecdotes. He had names for certain "hot spots" as he called them, and he would visit them frequently. One such area was "The Diaper" where he found some very unique items, including an old diaper someone had tossed out. Thus the location became known as "The Diaper". That was Dub's humorous way. He was quite the storyteller, always wore a warm welcoming smile, and always made everybody's day when he visited the Fort. He has since moved to Tomball, Texas, to be near family and everyone at Fort Chadbourne misses his weekly visits.

Dewey Chesnut, the other half of "Dub and Dewey" moved to Granbury, Texas, several years ago to be near his family as well. Like Dub, Dewey had a witty and friendly personality. Between these two, one was always trying to outdo the other. Dub played off Dewey, and Dewey off Dub. Dewey was out and about one day without Dub, and made a big discovery, a large Native American cache of flint tools located here on the Chadbourne Ranch. Story goes Dub was none too happy to be left out of that little adventure.

The miraculous cache Dewey found, consisted of some forty-nine flint pieces, believed to be over six thousand years old. It was an awesome addition to the Fort Chadbourne Native American Collection, and is presently on display in the Visitor's Center.

Sadly, Dewey passed away in December 2009. A memorial for he, and his wife Eloise, was held at Fort Chadbourne in June 2010.

Not many days go by that someone doesn't bring up a "Dub and Dewey" tale. Both will always be fondly remembered, and be a huge part of Fort Chadbourne history.

Without the volunteers, the donors, and the foundations that have graciously supported the efforts of the Fort Chadbourne Foundation, the goal would have taken much longer. In a ten year time frame the work has been achieved with only $6,500.00 received from a governmental agency, as a matching grant from The Texas Historical Commission. The remainder has come from very generous private foundations, and of course, personal donors, who have continued to donate and stand beside the Foundation throughout the years. Thanks and appreciations are due each one of them, including the following: Dodge Jones Foundation, Summerlee Foundation, Summerfield G. Roberts Foundation, Konczak Foundation, Concho

Valley RC&D, O'Donnell Foundation, NRA Foundation, Bronte Economic Development Board, and James Kenney for his Medal of Honor Collection. Also, David Carter and Rusty Spur Productions, for his production of the video, "The Lost Fort", narrated by Barry Corbin, which was filmed at Fort Chadbourne, and surrounding areas of Texas. The forty-five minute video is an amazing portrayal of life as it existed at Fort Chadbourne in the 1850's. And, last but not least, the Roberta Cole Johnson Estate.

In November 2009, the biggest dream of all, breaking ground on a new 12,500 square foot, two million dollar Visitor's Center came true. This structure houses all the unique artifacts, along with a fabulous antique gun collection including Sharps, Winchesters, Colts, and many other historic items. Displays from cannons to clothing, ranching history, Native American exhibits, and Medal of Honor displays are all there. Also included in the facility is a large research library, a gift shop, and administrative offices. Even a large covered pavilion for outdoor events makes this new facility a state of the art.

The building honors Roberta Cole Johnson, a lady who never laid eyes on Fort Chadbourne, but for now will ever be a part of its history. Mrs. Johnson passed away in 2008, leaving her estate in the hands of Charles and Joy Blake, her next door neighbors for many years. Charles and Joy who were members of the Concho Valley Archeological Society, and actually helped on several archeological excavations at Fort Chadbourne in the past, called one day with the earth shattering news. Mrs. Johnson had requested that her estate be distributed at the Blake's discretion. The only stipulation she bestowed on it, was it be given to non-profit organizations where the Blake's felt the money could best be used.

Roberta Cole Johnson
Portrait By: Jo Millican

When you work in non profit, you learn very quickly nothing comes easy. Normally money does not walk in the door unannounced. So, the greatest homage you can pay to an organization like the Fort Chadbourne Foundation is to give an unsolicited donation. In doing so, it shows the foundation has gained the respect of others in their endeavors, and has in some way made others want to be a part of their dream. There is no greater compliment than this.

Charles and Joy Blake

Groundbreaking Ceremony 2009

It is doubtful Joy and Charles Blake will ever fully realize the great impact they have made to this small rural community. Fort Chadbourne was not their only objective. Besides sharing the wealth in Mrs. Johnson's home town of Brenham, Texas, their gifts refurbished, and or built new churches in Bronte and Robert Lee, and aided in ongoing restoration of the 1907 Coke County jail. For many years these gifts will perpetually stimulate Coke County, and without their generosity, many of these exciting additions may never have been possible.

The Fort Chadbourne Foundation hosts Fort Chadbourne Days, a living history event, the first weekend of May. All local and area schools, are invited to attend free of charge. It has become a big event. As many as three hundred reenactors volunteer their time to bring Fort Chadbourne back to life as an 1850's military post. There are artillery, infantry, and cavalry drills along with hay rides to see the Fort Chadbourne buffalo herd, a black powder shoot, sutlers, buffalo hunters, Native American displays, antique gun displays, spinners, cowboys, live entertainment, and so much more. All of this free to schools and students on Friday. In 2009, Fort Chadbourne made a decision to forgo an entry fee even on Saturday when the general public is admitted, although, donations are graciously accepted.

The Fort Chadbourne Foundation never wants anyone to be turned away because of an unaffordable entry fee. To the foundation, preserving history and presenting it to the people who pass through its doors is a goal they have set, and hope to maintain.

The third Saturday of each September, the Fort Chadbourne Foundation has its annual fundraiser. A dinner show, along with auctions is the main attraction, and at this time, serves as the one and only monetary fundraising event a year. So the volunteer and donors that continue to support this non-profit organization are the backbone of much of the success one sees today. As long as these efforts continue, every attempt will be made to open the doors of Fort Chadbourne freely to all who are interested in Texas History. The foundation is mighty proud of what they have been able to achieve, and enjoy showing it off. They should be proud. It is truly an amazing fete.

In 1852, Fort Chadbourne became a military post on the frontier of Texas, and in 1877, it became a families enduring heritage. On April 2, 1973, Fort

Chadbourne was entered into the Register of Historic Places and was then afforded the privilege granted under the Historic Preservation Act of 1966. At that time, even though its potential was realized, and it was designated a historic place from the past, it stood in ruins. No one knew that in 1999 the beginning of a dream would once again begin to brighten the landscape of Texas. Its newly restored military buildings would once again stand proud, along with the only newly restored Butterfield Stage Station in the State of Texas. And, The Chadbourne Ranch, a family legacy, whose ancestor's had seen its potential as far back as the 1800's. Today it is still as much a part of this historic adventure as the fort itself. A hope and dream turned into reality. The soldiers who rode into Fort Chadbourne in 1852, to establish this Post, and Thomas Lawsom Odom, who built an everlasting heritage for his family here, would be very proud of the remarkable events that have transpired since the foundations inception in 1999.

Because of the tireless work of Lana and Garland Richards, the Foundation, and its many donors and volunteers, Fort Chadbourne, and Chadbourne Ranch, will now and forever be a part of

Texas History. May it always stand as proud in the future, as it did in the past, and as it does today.

BEFORE: East Barracks at Fort Chadbourne 2001

In 1852 there were plans for five sets of barracks. In all actuality, only two sets of barracks were completed, and three extra foundations. Two foundations are found east of this barracks, and one west of the stabilized barracks ruin. Those foundations are barely visible today. Between the years of 1852 to 1867 post returns show as few as 50 men, or as many as 450 men were stationed here at one time. Graffiti names and dates of soldiers appear on the outside walls of several of the buildings including Albert Haneman, Oct 19, 1858. In recent years his ancestors visited the Fort after reading about their Grandfathers 1858 inscription still visible today.

DURING: East Barracks at Fort Chadbourne 2002

The above photograph shows the procedure used to reconstruct the east enlisted men's barracks. Although, Garland Richards was told he needed to tear down this structure by a historical architect, he refused. His ingenuity and diligence, to perfect a way to use braces and turnbuckles in order to straighten and stabilize the crooked and crumbling walls, earned him recognition. In February 2003, he was awarded the Preservation Texas Award.

AFTER: East Barracks at Fort Chadbourne

In 2003, work was completed on the east barracks walls and roof. In 2004, a wood floor was added, followed by a porch on the front. With completion of the Visitor's Center in 2011, the barracks used for meetings and events since 2004, will be furnished to represent an enlisted soldier's home, as it would have been on the frontier, in the 1850's. Each barracks also had a detached kitchen built of logs or canvas, which stood directly behind the buildings. Archeological evidence at Fort Chadbourne proved this to be correct. In 2006, Jim Bruseth and Bill Pierson, with the Texas Historical Commission, performed a magnetometer survey on this area.

BEFORE: Officer's Quarter "Fountain House" 2001

The Officer's Quarters was nicknamed the "Fountain House" after a family with that name resided there during the ranching years. On several documents still in the family's possession today, a man by the name of Fountain witnessed Garland Odom's signature on several records. This building was also rumored to have been the quarters Robert E. Lee was to reside in when he was ordered to command Fort Chadbourne. At the last minute, his orders were changed, and he was placed in charge of Camp Cooper.

AFTER: Officer's Quarters "Fountain House"

Finished in 2002, this Officer's Quarters has become one of the most popular restored buildings on the tour. The inside walls make this quarters very unique. During its years, as a military and ranching building, more than fifty people have scratched their names on its walls. The oldest name with date appears to be 1875. Some names such as C. E. Butrick, Tecumseh, Michigan have been researched through census, and followed Mr. Butrick through his time in Texas, Arizona, California, and Alaska. Other graffiti, such as Red Horse 1875, who was a Delaware scout, and known to be here during that time period, appears inside one doorway. All of this was able to be saved during restoration.

BEFORE: Double Officer's Quarters 1923

The Double Officer's Quarters served the military, but it was also used for many years after that, as the ranch headquarters. Garland and Lucinda Odom were calling this home, when a fire broke out on September 24, 1919, destroying most of the structure. Only a piano was believed to be saved from the fire. In 2007, when archeological excavations were conducted, over 300,000 artifacts were recovered. Some pieces of burned and broken china bore the signature of Edna Odom, daughter of Garland and Lucinda. She hand painted china as a hobby, and the family, even today, still possess several of her hand painted china pieces.

AFTER: Double Officer's Quarters 2007

The officer's quarters are now a beautifully restored structure, with a dogtrot in between. They are furnished with many of the family heirlooms belonging to the Odom's, and decorated as a ranching home of the 1870's. The inside walls are plastered in a way to reveal the old existing rock walls of the ruin, while covering the newer added walls with plaster as it would have been done in the 1850's. This way those who tour, are able to visualize how much work goes into the actual reconstruction, and how the existing ruins are stabilized, keeping the historic value of the building.

BEFORE: Butterfield Stage Station 2008

Little was left of the Butterfield Stage Stop when work began in 2008. Archeological investigations were done, and along with the large foundation, five rooms and three fireplaces were located. It also revealed the Stage Stop had wooden floors. The west room received the travelers for meals, the middle room housed the station keeper, and the east end was used to store tack, serve the stagecoaches, horses, or mules. Over 40,000 artifacts were located including metal trunk pieces, coins, military and civilian buttons, saddle parts, several hand forged tools, tack, and eating utensils.

AFTER: Butterfield Stage Station 2009

The above photograph is taken from the south side, which depicts the backside of the Butterfield building. In 1858, the Butterfield Stage Stop had a corral on the east end, and the stages were received along the north side of the building. A photograph taken in the early 1900's revealed the staggered roofline, so it was implemented in the reconstruction. A ribbon cutting was held at Fort Chadbourne in November 2009, opening the only restored Butterfield Stage Stop in the State of Texas. The Stage Stop contains displays of a stagecoach and buggies, along with other frontier travel information.

BEFORE: *This root cellar was also used as a United States Post Office until 1906*

AFTER: *Root Cellar after stabilization 2002*

Fort Chadbourne Visitor's Center

Architect – Conda Richards

The above photograph depicts the new 12,500 square foot facility scheduled to open summer 2011. It houses an antique gun collection and an antique bar donated by Elaine and Wade Clifton. In the early 1900's many a cowboy stood at this bar in the Zappe Saloon, which was located in Ballinger, Texas. Other displays include thousands of Military Artifacts, Cannons, Native American, Ranching, Cowboy, and Medal of Honor Displays, along with a Media Center, a 1,250 sq. ft. Research Library, Gift Shop, and Administrative Offices. The background shows the Butterfield Stage Station, Barracks, and Officer's Quarters. An Eclipse windmill also on display in front of the Visitor's Center was rebuilt and moved from another part of the ranch.

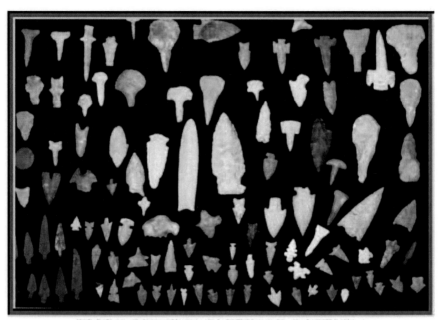

Native American & Military Artifacts

on display at Fort Chadbourne Visitor's Center

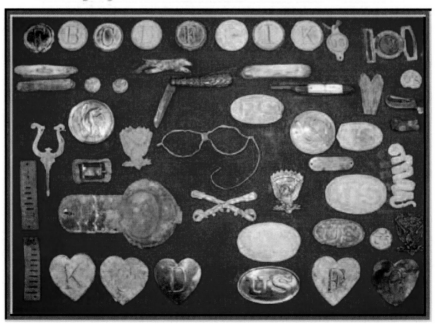

Gun pieces from Army & Navy Colt pistols have been found during excavations, along with some Sharps rifle pieces. Actual guns shown in display are used as reference examples only. Other military items below.

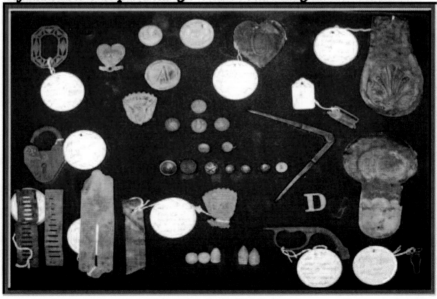

277

In 2010, new signage at the highway, along with a 30 foot spur was added to the entrance of Fort Chadbourne. The spur was designed after an 1850's cavalry spur that is on display in the Visitor's Center.

Fort Chadbourne Foundation
Officers and Directors

Garland Richards – President

Lana Richards – Secretary/Treasurer

Board of Directors

Kelly Gill – Abilene, TX

Tom Perini – Buffalo Gap, TX

September Daniel – Fort Worth, TX

Ann Pate – Blackwell, TX

Gay Frazer – Dallas, TX

Suzanne Campbell – San Angelo, TX

David Carter – Richland Hills, TX

Beverly Reeves – Clyde, TX

Ex Officio's

Pat Lee – Bronte, TX

Ronnie Poehls – Winters, TX

W. T. Davis – Tomball, TX

Kennie Mathews – Houston, TX

In Memory

R. L. Flannigan

Mary Frances Glenn   Dewey Chesnut

Chapter XXIV

Hot Off the Press!

What is printed in a newspaper today will most likely be a part of a historian's research in years to come. Most of us would agree many articles in print, whether it is those written today or way back when, are not always 100 per cent factual, but most are based on actual incidents if sometimes overly exaggerated. Needless to say, many of you may enjoy reading some of the newspaper clippings of old, and since they pertain to Fort Chadbourne they did become a part of its history.

February 12, 1854: The Texas News

A United States Army expedition under Captain John Page left San Antonio today to survey a suitable route for a transcontinental railroad. The soldiers will follow the route blazed a few years ago by Captain

Randolph B. Marcy, from Fort Chadbourne to Big Spring and then on to Fort Belknap. Captain Pope has instruction to investigate the possibility of drilling artesian wells throughout the Staked Plains while making his survey.

July 29, 1854: Texas State Gazette, Austin

The Fort Chadbourne troops at this point are likely to experience a little inconvenience for the want of meat rations. The contractors, Messrs. Gooch and McKay, recently lost the whole of their cattle by the depredations of the Comanche's who suddenly made a descent upon the Rancho and drove the cattle off.

October 25, 1854: Daily National Intelligencer, Washington

We are much pained that Fort Chadbourne, with its garrison of about fifty men, under the command of Captain Patrick Calhoun, of the 2nd dragoons, is considered as in imminent danger of an attack from the Comanche's, amounting to five or six hundred warriors, assembled in its neighborhood. These Indians will not in all probability suffer so fine an opportunity for theft and murder to pass; and we greatly fear that we may soon have to chronicle the massacre of several valuable officers and the men under their charge, with the loss of destruction of a considerable amount of public property.

The information is derived from a letter from Captain Calhoun to Major Neighbors, the famous Indian Agent in Texas, and it communicates the painful and humiliating fact that such is the absence of any feeling of respect for the force at Fort Chadbourne among the Comanches, and such the entire powerlessness of its gallant commander, as brave an officer we know as any in the service, to enforce respect, that the savages had at the date of the last letter attached and wounded one of the garrison the previous night within a few hundred yards of the Fort. How heartily we wish that Captain Calhoun had then had the hundred men that he wanted that he might have carried, in his words, "the war into Africa!"

March 7, 1855: Trenton State Gazette

An expedition consisting of two companies of Dragoons and three companies of Rangers commanded by Captain Calhoun has set out from Fort Chadbourne to operate against the Southern Comanches of Texas. A train number 63 government wagons, laden with supplies, accompanied the expedition.

June 14, 1856: San Antonio Texian

On the 14th express reached San Antonio which left Fort Chadbourne on the 8th bringing the unwelcome news of the inhuman murder and capture of two express riders, who were on their way from Fort McKavett to Fort Chadbourne. It seems that the two men had arrived within forty miles of Fort Chadbourne when they were attacked probably by a large number of Comanches, overpowered and killed. One of the bodies has since been found; the head was severed from the body, one leg was cut off at the knee, and the body otherwise mangled in the most horrible manner. The body of the other express rider up to our going to press has not been found.

June 28, 1856 – Cherokee Sentinel

Texas Western Railroad company, colonel A. Gray, the engineer of this company, who made the survey to San Diego some two years since, from Fort Chadbourne, passed through our city on Sunday last, on his return to Washington. His present operations (just concluded) have been to fix the latitudes of 32°.

On the Trinity and Brazos, and correcting his former work between Fort Chadbourne and the eastern border of the State in the direction of Shreveport, La., with barometrical and other instrumental observations, necessary to a complete and accurate profile of the route.

August 15, 1858 – Dallas Weekly Herald

Mr. King, Esquire reports that two coaches with horses passed through Fort Belknap to be deposited at Fort Chadbourne ready for use on the California mail route on the 15th of next month.

February 16, 1859 – Dallas Weekly Herald

A train of eight wagons with twelve oxen in each passed through town last week, loaded with flour for the government troops at Fort Chadbourne. The wagons contained some 40,000 lbs of flour, furnished by Mr. W. H. Witt, Proprietor of the Trinity mills in this county. It is put in under the contract of Mr. A. J. Mackey of Fort Chadbourne.

September 2, 1859 – San Francisco Bulletin

At Hardy's Station, Fort Chadbourne, Ham, the station house keeper, shot a stage driver name Lowe, who died in three hours. Cause of difficulty unknown.

May 7, 1860 – New York Herald

Private advices from Fort Chadbourne state that the Indians in this vicinity have cut off the mountain pass mail station on the Butterfield Overland Route, killing three men and two boys, stealing mules and slaughtering the cattle of the company. Captain Wallace commandant at Chadbourne sent his men out twenty five miles to the station to bury the dead and take charge of the effects until the employers of the company should arrive. Captain Wallace represents the recent outrages on the part of the Indians on this route as unusually daring.

August 29, 1867 – San Antonio Express

We are glad to learn that General Hatch, who is in command of the Fourth United States Cavalry contemplates inaugurating a new plan of frontier defense, making Fort McKavett his headquarters, and scattering his forces along a line of defense from Fort Clark to Fort Chadbourne, and scouting over the entire distance. This will form an out line of defense.

November 30, 1867 – San Antonio Express

Notice-Wanted: Depot Quartermaster's Office, San Antonio, Texas. Wanted at the Deport

Quartermaster's office: 2 experienced engineers, 2 experienced surveyors, 18 laborers. For service at Fort Chadbourne. Particulars can be had on application. J. G. Lee, Brevet Lt. Colonel and A.Q.M., U. S. Army.

October 27, 1870 – San Antonio Express

Notice: The undersigned having qualified as Executrix of the estate of Samuel A. Maverick, deceased, hereby gives notice to all persons indebted to said estate, to come forward and settle the same; and to all persons having claims against said estate to present them for approval within one year from the fourth day of October, 1870, being the date of the probating of the will of Samuel A. Maverick, deceased. Signed: Mary A. Maverick, San Antonio, October 27, 1870.

February 11, 1885- Dallas Daily Herald

Sweetwater, February 10 (Special) – A Witness Killed – At 8:30 tonight B. T. Warren, who was formerly a ranger, and later in the employ of Col. T. L. Odom, and a prominent witness against parties residing in this county, who stand charged in the district court of Runnells County with fence-cutting, while sitting in the office of the Central Hotel, in this place, was shot and instantly killed by some unknown party. The shot was fired from the street. Certain parties are suspected, but there is no proof positive yet.

February 14, 1885 – Dallas Daily Herald

In reference to the killing of Ben Warren, at this place, on the night of the 10th, it should be stated that there have been quite a number of parties residing in the extreme southern part of this county, some thirty miles from town, indicted in Runnels County for fence cutting, principally upon the evidence of Ben Warren. The fence cut belonged to Col. T. Odom & Co., and there existed an ill feeling between the parties known as fence-cutters and the owners of the fence. On the day of the murder of warren, he had been tried in the county court of this county for maliciously killing a cow and W. J. Wood and Riley Hilton were the principal witnesses against him. The jury failed to agree. Warren had been at a former term of the court convicted of the charge fine $200.00. This was his second trial and the truth of the condition is, there was a feud existing between the parties. On the next morning after the killing, W. C. Steele, just of the peace, held an inquest over the body, and the jury after eighteen hours earnest investigation, came to the conclusion that W. J. Wood and Neil Barrett were the guilty parties and they are now in jail. Their examining trial is to come on Monday next.

May 3, 1890 – Dallas Morning News

Garland Odom had his buggy upset on his way to Abilene, and was thrown out and considerably bruised, coming near having his neck dislocated. He is about this morning, but carries his head one-sided.

September 26, 1919 – Dallas Morning News

Ballinger, Texas, Sept 25 - The building formerly occupied as officer's quarters at Fort Chadbourne, thirty miles northwest of here, was destroyed by fire yesterday afternoon. The building was constructed in 1854. In 1877 Colonel G. G. Odom purchased the property and converted the building into a ranch house. Colonel Odom and family were occupying the fort when it was destroyed and lost family relics over 100 years old.

January 5, 1901 – The Ballinger Banner – Leader

One of the most unique and delightful entertainments ever given in Ballinger was tendered the young people Saturday night by Miss Clara and

Neil Guion. It was a "Bellamy" party and to those not posted as to what a Bellamy party was, it was explained that the guest were expected to attend dressed backwards. Those present included Edna Odom and Conda Wylie.

Troop Rosters

Federal Troops

NAME	RANK	REGIMENT
Adams, W. C.	Lt.	
Alexander, Lewis	Pvt.	8th Infantry
Alexander, R. H.	Asst. Surgeon	Medical
Algon, Walter J.		2nd Dragoons
Allen, Robert	Pvt.	1st Infantry
Alm, Charles	Pvt.	2nd Dragoons
Anderson, George B.	2nd Lt.	2nd Dragoons
Anderson, Richard H.	2nd Lt.	2nd Dragoons
Anderson, W. W.	Asst. Surgeon	Medical
Anderson, W. A.	Pvt.	4th Cavalry
Armstrong, Frances	2nd Lt.	2nd Dragoons
Arthur, Benjamin H.	Capt.	1st Infantry
Babcock, William H.	Asst. Surgeon	Medical
Bagby, Arthur	2nd Lt.	8th Infantry
Baharns, Thomas	Pvt.	2nd Dragoon
Bainbridge	Col.	
Balmur, John	Bugler	4th Cavalry
Bangs, Richard	Pvt.	2nd Dragoons
Banquo, Alexander	Pvt.	1st Infantry
Barber, George C.	2nd Lt.	8th Infantry
Barris, Willis	Pvt.	2nd Cavalry
Bartlett, Edward	Wagonneer	4th Cavalry
Barton, Seth M.	Capt.	1st Infantry
Battie, James	Pvt.	3rd Infantry
Bayliss, William C.	2nd Lt.	4th Cavalry
Beardsley, John	2nd Lt.	8th Infantry
Beaumont, Eugene B.***	Lt. Col.	4th Cavalry
Beeson, John	Corp.	6th Cavalry
Belger, James	Major	
Bennett, Lamar M.	Drummer	8th Infantry
Bierbank, Sidney	Major	1st Infantry
Biggs, Herman	Lt.	

Soldiers Roster Continued-

Bigham, James S.	2nd Lt.	TMR*
Blake, C.	1st Lt.	8th Infantry
Bliss, Zenas R.***	2nd Lt.	8th Infantry
Boehm, Peter M.***	1st Lt.	4th Cavalry
Boggess, Giles S.	Capt.	TMV**
Bomell, George	Pvt.	3rd Infantry
Bradfute, William R.	Capt.	2nd Cavalry
Brien, John	Pvt.	2nd Dragoons
Brooks, Lewis D.	Drummer	8th Infantry
Burchill, Walter	Pvt.	4th Cavalry
Burke, John	Pvt.	4th Cavalry
Calhoun, Patrick	Capt.	2nd Dragoons
Callehan, James	1st Lt.	4th Cavalry
Cameron, John	Pvt.	8th Calvary
Carroll, William	Pvt.	4th Cavalry
Carrott, Andrew	Pvt.	4th Cavalry
Caston, James K.P.	Trumpeter	4th Cavalry
Chaddin, Samuel		Guide
Cherry, Samuel		Guide
Clympton, Joseph	Col.	1st Infantry
Cody, Michael	Pvt.	3rd Infantry
Cole, Robert G.	2nd Lt.	8th Infantry
Collatin, James	Hosp. Steward	Medical
Collins, Hugh	Pvt.	4th Cavalry
Cone, Aurelius F.	2nd Lt.	1st Infantry
Cosby, George B.	1st Lt.	2nd Cavalry
Cox, Daniel		Recruit
Cracey		No Info
Craswell, W. A.	Asst. Surg.	Medical
Cummings, Thomas	Pvt.	3rd Infantry
Cunningham, Michael	Pvt.	2nd Cavalry
Cunningham, George	2nd Lt.	2nd Cavalry
Daugherty, Francis M.	1st Lt.	TMV
Davenport, Julius	Pvt.	4thCavalry
Davis, John	Pvt.	8th Infantry
Dodge, Richard J.	2nd Lt.	8th Infantry
Dohang, John	Pvt.	1st Infantry
Donoghue, Darl	Fifer	8th Infantry

Soldiers Roster Continued-

Dougherty, Peter	Pvt.	4th Cavalry
Dreseler, Augustus A.	Sgt.	4th Cavalry
Dufey, Daniel	Pvt.	1st Infantry
Dumreicher, Conrad C.	Asst. Surg.	Medical
Dunbar, John	Pvt.	2nd Dragoons
Eagle, Robert N.		2nd Cavalry
Eastman, Seth	Capt.	1st Infantry
Elmre, Thomas T.	Pvt.	4th Cavalry
Ethier, Anthony	Pvt.	2nd Dragoons
Evans, Nathan	Capt.	2nd Cavalry
Faurier, William W.	Pvt.	4th Cavalry
Field, Charles W.	2nd Lt.	2nd Dragoons
Fink, Theodore	2nd Lt.	8th Infantry
Fitzhugh, William	Capt.	TMV
Flagherty, Patrick	Pvt.	1st Infantry
Follet, Frederick M.	2nd Lt.	8th Infantry
Foster, Charles	Sgt.	4th Cavalry
Gallagher, Patrick	Corp.	1st Infantry
Gardner, Louis	Sgt.	4th Cavalry
Garland, John	Brig. Gen.	8th Infantry
Garrard, Kenner	1st Lt.	2nd Cavalry
Garrety, John	Pvt.	6th Cavalry
Garrison, Caleb J.	2nd Lt.	TMV
Geisel, Andrew	Pvt.	4th Cavalry
Geisel, John	2nd Lt.	1st Infantry
Gilbert, Charles C.	1st Lt.	1st Infantry
Givens, Newton C.	Lt.	2nd Dragoon
Graff, Adam	Corp.	1st Infantry
Gray, Francis	Pvt.	5th Infantry
Greene, Mathew	Pvt.	3rd Infantry
Haepin, James	Pvt.	3rd Infantry
Hagans, James	Sgt.	1st Infantry
Haldeman, Horace	2nd Lt.	8th Infantry
Halihan, John	Pvt.	1st Infantry
Hamlet, John	Pvt.	6th Cavalry
Hanlon, Thomas	Fifer	
Haneman, Albert	Bugler	2nd Cavalry
Hanson, William H.	Pvt.	4th Cavalry

Soldiers Roster Continued-

Hardee, William J.	Lt. Col.	2nd Dragoons
Harris, Guy	Corp.	4th Cavalry
Harvey, William S.	Col.	2nd Dragoons
Hawes, John M.	1st Lt.	2nd Dragoons
Hays, Daniel	Pvt.	8th Infantry
Hedges, Joseph***	Capt.	4th Cavalry
Hemphill, William	1st Lt.	4th Cavalry
Henninger, Henry	Pvt.	3rd Infantry
Henshaw, John C.	Major	7th Infantry
Herman, John	Pvt.	2nd Dragoon
Hettler, Jocob	Fifer	8th Infantry
Hick, William H.	2nd Lt.	4th Cavalry
Higgins, Andrew	Pvt.	4th Cavalry
Hills, Edward P.	Hosp. Stew.	Medical
Hogg, Charles	Pvt.	4th Cavalry
Holabird, Samuel B.	1st Lt.	1st Infantry
Holliday, Jonas P.	1st Lt.	2nd Dragoons
Holloway, Edmunds B	1st Lt.	8th Infantry
Holman, James H.	2nd Lt.	1st Infantry
Hood, John B.	2nd Lt	2nd Cavalry
Horstman, John	Pvt.	8th Infantry
Howland, William	Fifer	8th Infantry
Huntt, G. G.	Capt.	4th Cavalry
Irwin, David A.	1st Lt.	4th Cavalry
Irwin, John G.	1st Sgt.	2nd Dragoons
Jenifer, Walter H.	1st Lt.	2nd Cavalry
Johnson, Dudley	Ord. Sgt.	
Johnson, John	Pvt.	4th Cavalry
Johnson, Orlando D.	Sgt.	4th Cavalry
Jones, William	Sgt.	4th Cavalry
Kane, John	Pvt.	3rd Infantry
Kealy, W. R.	Pvt.	2nd Cavalry
Keenman, Joseph F.	Pvt.	4th Cavalry
Kelly, Edward	Fifer	8th Infantry
Kelly, Thomas	Pvt.	2nd Dragoons
Kelly, Michael J.	Major	4th Cavalry
Kennedy, Robert	Pvt.	4th Cavalry

Soldiers Roster Continued–

Keogh, Miles W.	2nd Lt.	4th Cavalry
Kerr, George	Pvt.	2nd Dragoons
Ketchum, William H.	Drummer	8th Infantry
King, John H.	Capt.	1st Infantry
Kinley, Edward	Pvt.	4th Cavalry
Kunzell, Frederick	Pvt.	3rd Infantry
Lane, John	Pvt.	3rd Infantry
Langworthy, Elisha P.	Asst. Surg.	Medical
Larson, James	1st Sgt.	4th Cavalry
Laughlin, John	Drummer	8th Infantry
Lazelle	2nd Lt.	
Lear, Elijah	Pvt.	8th Infantry
Lecrist, Robert B.	Pvt.	4th Cavalry
Lee, Arthur Tracy	Capt.	8th Infantry
Lee, John	1st Lt.	4th Cavalry
Limons, J.	Asst. Surg.	Medical
Longstreet, James	1st Lt.	8th Infantry
Lowe, William W.	2nd Lt.	2nd Dragoons
Lynch, Thomas	1st Inf.	1st Infantry
Madden, Samuel	Drummer	8th Infantry
Maroney, John	Pvt.	4th Cavalry
Marshall, Henry	Sgt.	2nd Dragoons
Marshall, Louis H.	2nd Lt.	3rd Infantry
Martin, Frederick D.	Pvt.	4th Cavalry
Matlock, Ruben	Pvt.	2nd Dragoons
May, E. S.	Pvt.	3rd Infantry
McCormick, C.	Surg.	Medical
McCoulskey, Patrick	Pvt.	3rd Infantry
McDermitt, Charles	Pvt.	2nd Dragoons
McDermitt, Martin	Pvt.	2nd Dragoons
McDougall, John	Sgt.	4th Cavalry
McGregg, David	2nd Lt.	2nd Dragoons
McIntosh, Alexander	Drummer	8th Infantry
McIntosh, James	2nd Lt.	8th Infantry
McFalls, Thaddeus B.	Post Chaplain	
McLean, Eugene E.	1st Lt.	1st Infantry
Merchant, Charles G.	1st Lt.	8th Infantry

Soldiers Roster Continued-

Midean, G. G.	Capt.	
Miller, Andrew G.	1st Lt.	1st Infantry
Miner, John	Hosp. Stew.	Medical
Miror, John	Pvt.	2n Dragoons
Michell, Tobias H.	Post Chaplain	
Monroe, Biggs		
Montgomery, John	Pvt.	2nd Dragoons
Montgomery, William	Capt.	8th Infantry
Moore, James	Pvt.	1st Infantry
Moore, Tredwell	1st Lt.	2nd Infantry
Morris, Gouveneur	Lt. Col.	1st Infantry
Morris, George	Pvt.	4th Cavalry
Morrison, Pitcairn	Major	8th Infantry
Morrow, William	Surg.	Medical
Murphy, Arthur	Pvt.	1st Infantry
Murray, James H.	Pvt.	4th Cavalry
Newhouse, Charles	Sgt.	4th Cavalry
Newton, Washington	Capt.	2nd Dragoons
Nixon, John	Pvt.	3rd Infantry
Oakes, James	Capt.	2nd Dragoons
O'Brien, John	Pvt.	1st Infantry
O'Brien, Henry	Sgt.	4th Cavalry
O"Caltaphan, Thomas H.	Pvt.	3rd Infantry
O'Connell, William	Capt.	4th Cavalry
O'Donnell, Michael	Pvt.	3rd Infantry
O'Donnell, John	Corp.	3rd Infantry
Palfrey, Edward A.	2nd Lt.	7th Infantry
Palmer, Innis	Capt.	2nd Cavalry
Parker, Alanzo	Pvt.	3rd Infantry
Parker, James C.	Pvt.	4th Cavalry
Partridge, Michael	Pvt.	1st Infantry
Patty, William	Pvt.	8th Infantry
Phillipp, Farley	Pvt.	4th Cavalry
Phillips, Edwin D.	1st Lt.	1st Infantry
Phillips, Isaac J.	Pvt.	5th Infantry
Pickens, Thomas C.	1st Lt.	8th Infantry
Pickett, George C.	Capt.	8th Infantry

Soldiers Roster Continued-

Pilgrim, William	Pvt.	4th Cavalry
Pitcher, Thomas G.	1st Lt.	8th Infantry
Pleasanton, Alfred	1st Lt.	2nd Dragoons
Porter, A. Parker	2nd Lt.	2nd Cavalry
Potter, Albert	Pvt.	4th Cavalry
Powers, William	Pvt.	2nd Dragoons
Pratt, Josiah J.	Corp.	4th Cavalry
Pyler, Charles H.	2nd Lt.	2nd Dragoons
Quick, Jesse	Recruit	
Quinlan, Patrick	Pvt.	2nd Cavalry
Randal, Horace	2nd Lt.	Mt. Rifleman
Rawon, Frederick	Pvt.	3rd Infantry
Reeves, Charles H.	Pvt.	2nd Dragoons
Reynolds, A. W.	Capt.	
Reynolds, John H.	Pvt.	4th Cavalry
Reynolds, Samuel	1st Lt.	1st Infantry
Rhymard, George	Fifer	8th Infantry
Rogers, Edwin W.	2nd Lt.	TMV
Rogers, Patrick H.	Capt.	TMV
Rot, John	Drummer	8th Infantry
Ross, John	Drummer	8th Infantry
Ross, Martin	Pvt.	8th Infantry
Ruggles, George D.	2nd Lt.	1st Infantry
Schaafer, Frederick	Pvt.	4th Cavalry
Scott	Pvt.	1st Infantry
Scott, Alexander H.	Pvt.	4th Cavalry
Scott, Douglas M.	2nd Lt.	4th Cavalry
Seawell, Washington	Lt. Col.	8th Infantry
Selden, Joseph	Capt.	8th Infantry
Shaffer, Robert	Fifer	8th Infantry
Shalers, Samuel	Pvt.	6th Cavalry
Sheld, John	Sgt.	1st Infantry
Sherburne, John P.	2nd Lt.	1st Infantry
Short, John	Pvt.	4th Cavalry
Simms, Henry W.	Pvt.	2nd Dragoons
Slane, Peter	Corp.	2nd Dragoons
Smith, C H.	Asst. Surg.	Medical

Soldiers Roster Continued-

Name	Rank	Unit
Smith, Edmund R.	Capt.	2nd Cavalry
Smith, Frances	Pvt.	1st Infantry
Smith, Joseph R.	Asst. Surg.	Medical
Smith, Larkin	Capt.	8th Infantry
Smith, Melancton	2nd Lt.	8th Infantry
Smith, Robert	Pvt.	3rd Infantry
Snelling, James	1st Lt.	8th Infantry
Souvet, Burket	Pvt.	2nd Cavalry
Squires, William	Drummer	8th Infantry
Stackpole, George	Pvt.	2nd Dragoons
Stanley, David S.***	2nd Lt.	2nd Dragoons
Steiner, J.M.	Asst. Surg.	Medical
Steinmitz, William	Sgt.	4th Cavalry
Steuart, George H.	2nd Lt.	2nd Dragoons
Stockton, Philip	2nd Lt.	8th Infantry
Swift, Ebenezer	Asst. Surg.	Medical
Taylor, G.	Major	
Taylor, John	Interpreter	
Thalers, Samuel	Pvt.	6th Cavalry
Thiess, Frederick	Pvt.	4th Cavalry
Thomas, Charles W.	2nd Lt.	1st Infantry
Thomas, John	Pvt.	4th Cavalry
Thompson, Henry	Fifer	8th Infantry
Thompson, Charles H.	Pvt.	4th Cavalry
Thurston, George A.	2nd Lt.	4th Cavalry
Tiellett, George E.	Capt.	8th Infantry
Todd, David K.	Pvt.	4th Cavalry
Toole, Peter		
Topping, Thomas	Drummer	8th Infantry
Torrence, Joseph		
Trussell, Andrew J.	2nd Lt.	TMV
Turk, Paul	Pvt.	2nd Dragoons
Tyler, C. H.	2nd Lt.	2nd Dragoons
Vallot, Peter	Fifer	8th Infantry
Van Dorn, Earl	Capt.	2nd Cavalry
Van Horn, Charles W.	Lt.	4th Cavalry
Vernon, Thomas	Sgt.	4th Cavalry

300

Soldiers Roster Continued-

Vernou, Charles A.	2nd Lt.	4th Cavalry
Wade, Orville B.	Asst. Surg.	TMV
Wagner, Frederick	Pvt.	6th Cavalry
Waite, Carlos A.	Col.	1st Infantry
Wallace, George W.	Capt.	1st Infantry
Washington, Thornton	2nd Lt.	1st Infantry
Watson, Augustus	Pvt.	4th Cavalry
Watts, William	Fifer	8th Infantry
Webb	Lt.	5th Infantry
Weisjer, Theodore	Pvt.	3rd Infantry
Wentzel, Louis G.	Pvt.	4th Cavalry
Wheeler	Lt.	2nd Cavalry
Wheeler, John	Pvt.	4th Cavalry
Willer, Andrew G.	Capt.	1st Infantry
Williams, John	Pvt.	4th Cavalry
Williams, Thomas G.	2nd Lt.	1st Infantry
Wilson, Joseph K.	Sgt.	8th Infantry
Wilson, H. K.	Pvt.	2nd Dragoons
Wilson, James	Pvt.	4th Cavalry
Winship, Oscar F.	Capt.	2nd Dragoons
Wint, Theodore J.	1st Lt.	4th Cavalry
Wood, Elia	1st Lt.	TMV
Wood, Henry C.***	2nd Lt.	1st Infantry
Wood, Lafayette B.	1st Lt.	8th Infantry
Woodson, George	Pvt.	2nd Dragoons
Wright, Alexander S.	1st Lt.	TMV
Wurm, Daniel	Pvt.	4th Cavalry

- List was taken from muster rolls and post returns.
- List may be incomplete.
- Spelling of names appear as they did on returns.
- Soldiers rank appears at time of service at Fort Chadbourne.

*   **Texas Mounted Rifles**
**   **Texas Mounted Volunteers**
*** **Medal of Honor Recipient**

Texas Regimental Troops

Roster of Soldiers, 1861 (incomplete)

NAME	RANK	REGIMENT
Bell, J. Thomas		
Bellamy, F. Asa	Pvt.	1st Cavalry
Bigham, James S	2nd Lt.	1st Cavalry
Davidson, Sidney G.	Capt.	1st Cavalry
Dereson, Jesse A	Surgeon	1st Cavalry
Franklin, Nathal J.	Blacksmith	1st Cavalry
Frost, F. C.	Lt. Col.	1st Cavalry
Frost, Thomas		1st Cavalry
Gallatin, Milam	Pvt.	1st Cavalry
Gallatin, Samuel		
Halley, R. B.		TMR*
Hamilton, D. Wiley	Pvt.	
Lane	Hosp. Stew.	TMR
Leath, Thomas	Pvt.	TMR
Ludlow, Henry	Pvt.	1st Cavalry
Mackey, M. Columbus	Pvt.	1st Cavalry
Marshall, James C.	Pvt.	TMR
Maverick, Samuel J.	Pvt.	1st Cavalry
McCulloch, Henry	Col.	1st Cavalry
McDaniel, James	Pvt.	1st Cavalry
McNair, Duncan	Corp.	TMR
Morris, B. Oliver	Pvt.	1st Cavalry
Morris, William	Pvt.	1st Cavalry
Naylor, Columbus	Pvt.	1st Cavalry
Pace, Edward	Pvt.	1st Cavalry
Pullen, Samuel J.	Pvt.	1st Cavalry
Rancier, Edwin	Sgt.	1st Cavalry
Roberts, Wade G.	Pvt.	1st Cavalry
Scott, Jeremiah D.	Sgt.	1st Cavalry
Scott, Robert M.	Pvt.	TMR
Shelton, Samuel	Pvt.	TMR
Warren, George	Pvt.	1st Cavalry

*Texas Mounted Rifles

"Mean Strength" recorded by Assistant Surgeons, U.S.A., while stationed at Fort Chadbourne October 1852-March 1861.

YEAR	MONTH	OFFICERS	ENLISTED MEN	TOTAL
1852	October	10	176	186
	November	7	130	137
	December	7	172	179
1853	January	7	156	163
	February	7	152	159
	March	8	163	171
	April	9	285	294
	May	8	261	269
	June	10	247	257
	July	10	256	266
	August	9	257	266
	September	7	144	151
	October	4	58	62
	November	3	84	87
	December	2	69	71
1854	January	2	44	46
	February	2	34	36
	March	2	39	41
	April	1 1/3	60 1/3	61 2/3
	May	1	64 2/3	65 2/3
	June	4	87 2/3	91 2/3
	July	5	84	89
	August	6	83	89
	September	8	103	111
	October	7	93	100
	November	7	92	99
	December	6	85	91
1855	January	10	199	209
	February	3	49	52
	March	4	56	60
	April	6	81	87
	May	4	83	87
	June	3	70	73
	July	3	78	81

YEAR	MONTH	OFFICERS	ENLISTED MEN	TOTAL
	August	5	111 2/3	116 2/3
	September	4	99 2/3	103 2/3
	October	3 2/3	98	101 2/3
	November	3 1/3	97	100 1/3
	December	4	99	103
1856	January	4	98	102
	February	4	141	145
	March	3 1/3	151	154 1/3
	April	3	150	153
	May	3	147	150
	June	4	131 1/3	135 1/3
	July	3 2/3	141 1/3	145
	August	3	140	143
	September	2 1/3	143	145 1/3
	October	3	152	155
	November	3	143	146
	December	5	162	167
1857	January	5	134	139
	February	5	131	136
	March	5	94	99
	April	5	94	99
	May	3	98	101
	June	5	89	94
	July	6	84	90
	August	6	85	91
	September	4	80	84
	October	4	79	84
	November	5	74	79
	December	4	72	76
1858	January	4	120	124
	February	3	148	151
	March	4	136	140
	April	4	151	155
	May	2	130	132

YEAR	MONTH	OFFICERS	ENLISTED MEN	TOTAL
	June	2	112	114
	July	2	112	114
	August	2	110	112
	September	1	76	77
	October	1	49	50
	November	1	39	40
	December	2	70	72
1859	January	3	75	78
	February	3	74	77
	March	4	83	87
	April	3	85	88
	May	3	82	85
	June	3	80	83
	July	3	72	75
	August	4	65	69
	September	4	59	63
	October	4	58	62
	November	5	58	63
	December	4	61	65
1860	January	4	61	65
	February	4	61	65
	March	4	56	60
	April	3	51	54
	May	3	72	75
	June	3	79	82
	July	4	87	91
	August	3	77	80
	September	5	77	82
	October	5	86	91
	November	6	87	94
	December	7	87	94
1861	January	5	89	94
	February	4	77	81
	March	5	77	82

Fort Chadbourne Commanders

Captain John Beardsley	October 1852
Captain Arthur Tracy Lee	November 1852
Captain John Beardsley	December 1852
Colonel John Garland	January 1853
Captain John Beardsley	March 1853
Major Pitcairn Morrison	June 1853
Lt. Col. Washington Seawell	July 1853
Bvt. Captain L. B. Wood	September 1853
1st Lt. James Hawes	October 1853
Asst. Surgeon Eben Swift	April 1854
Captain Patrick Calhoun	May 1854
1st Lt. Alfred Pleasonton	October 1854
Captain Patrick Calhoun	November 1854
1st Lt. James Hawes	March 1855
Captain Seth Eastman	August 1855
1st Lt. Charles Gilbert	March 1856
Captain Seth Eastman	April 1856
1st Lt. Andrew G. Miller	July 1856
Captain John H. King	February 1857
1st Lt. Andrew G. Miller	April 1857

Captain John H. King	May 1857
1st Lt. Thornton Washington	June 1857
Captain John H. King	July 1857
1st Lt. Samuel H. Reynolds	February 1858
Captain John H. King	March 1858
2nd Lt. Charles Thomas	May 1858
Captain John H. King	June 1858
Captain William Bradfute	August 1858
2nd Lt. Aurelius F. Cone	December 1858
Captain George Wallace	January 1859
Lt. Col. Gouverneur Morris	June 1860
Captain Robert B. Halley *	June 1861
Lt. Col. Thomas C. Frost *	June 1861
Captain Eugene Beaumont	May 1867
Captain G. G. Huntt	July 1867

* Texas Regimental Troops

Medal of Honor Recipients

Who Served at Fort Chadbourne

Beaumont, Eugene Beauharnais: 1837-1916

Post Commander 1867, 4th Cavalry – Co A

Medal of Honor – Civil War – Awarded: March 30, 1898

"Obtained permission from the corps commander to advance upon enemy's position with the 4th Cavalry, of which he was a lieutenant; led an attack upon a battery, dispersed the enemy and captured the guns. At Selman, AL, charged at the head of his regiment, into the second and last line of the enemy's works."

Bliss, Zenus Randall: 1835-1900

Served at Fort Chadbourne 1855, 8th Infantry – Co A

Medal of Honor – Civil War – Awarded: Dec. 30, 1898

"This officer, to encourage his regimen; which had never before been in action, and which had been ordered to lie down to protect itself from the enemy's fire, arose to his feet, advanced in front of the line, and himself fired several shots at the enemy at short range, being fully exposed to their fire at the time."

Boehm, Peter Martin: 1845-1914

Served at Fort Chadbourne 1867, 4th Cavalry, Co A

Medal of Honor – Civil War – Awarded Dec. 15, 1898

"While acting as aide to General Custer, took a flag from the hands of color bearer, rode in front of a line that was being driven back and, under a heavy fire, rallied the men, re-formed the line, and repulsed the charge."

Hedges, Joseph S.: 1836-1910

Served at Fort Chadbourne 1867, 4th Cavalry, Co D

Medal of Honor – Civil War – Awarded April 5, 1898

"At the head of his regiment charged a field battery with strong infantry support, broke the enemy's line and, with other mounted troops, captured 3 guns and many prisoners."

Stanley, David Sloane: 1828-1902

Served at Fort Chadbourne 1853, 2nd Dragoons, Co C

Medal of Honor – Civil War – Awarded March 29, 1893

"At a critical moment rode to the font of one of his brigades, reestablished its lines, and gallantly led it in a successful assault."

Wood, Henry Clay: 1832-1918

Served at Fort Chadbourne 1856, 1st Infantry, Co D

Medal of Honor – Civil War – Awarded October 23, 1893

"Distinguished gallantry."

Died at Fort Chadbourne

Last Name	First Name	Rank	Regiment	Company	Died	Notes
Algon *	Walter J.		2nd Dragoons	G	01-11-1855	Shot by Pvt. Chas. Alm
Arthur *	Benjamin H	Captain	1st Infantry	F	02-11-1856	Pneumonia, with gastritis and rheumatism
Bauer *	Louis	Pvt	1st Infantry	F	04-20-1856	Died
Cady ***	Robins	Pvt	1st Infantry	F	05-27-1856	Killed and Dismembered by Indians
Clark ***	John			D	09-19-1867	Yellow Fever - Buried Alexandria National Cemetary - Louisiana Died in Galveston
Collins	Hugh	Pvt	4th Cavalry	A	08-23-1867	Killed by Indians on the Concho.
Davis	Alexander B.				09-01-1855	Killed by Indians 14 miles from Fort Chadbourne
Ellis	James	Pvt	1st Infantry	F	09-14-1856	Drowned in San Saba River
Farrell *	Patrick	Pvt	1st Infantry	G	06-19-1860	Disease of Heart
Gibbert *	Martin	Pvt	1st Infantry	F	06-28-1856	Shot by sentinel who mistook him for an Indian
Haines *	John		1st Infantry	F	05-27-1856	Killed and Dismembered by Indians
Halihan *	John	Pvt	1st Infantry	A	12-18-1857	Trachealtis
Harr *	William	Pvt	4th Cavalry	A	1867	In confinement awaiting trial on desertion. Died of Yellow Fever
Hays *	Daniel	Pvt	8th Infantry	A	12-30-1853	Left sick in hospital when company received orders for Rio Grande. Phthisis Pulmonte
Herne *	Daniil	Pvt	1st Infantry	D	12-26-1856	Bronchitis
Higgins	Andrew		4th Cavalry	M	09-09-1867	Died in Austin
Hoffman *	John	Pvt	1st Cavalry	D	08-18-1855	Scorbutus - Lack of Vit. C
Kelly *	Michael J.	Captain	4th Cavalry	G	08-13-1867	Typhoid Fever
Kennedy *	John	Pvt		K	08-29-1853	Left by Company due to illness
Maloney *	Patrick	Pvt	8th Infantry	A	12-07-1852	Deserter who died shortly after arriving of Dysentary (Fort)
Maroney ***	John	Pvt		D	08-22-1867	Antonio Nat. Cem. Plot G/322
McCann *	William		1st Infantry	F	07-26-1856	Dropped Dead while on Guard Duty
McCoy *	Patrick	Pvt	1st Infantry	G	04-24-1859	Rebris Remittens (Fever)
McDougall	John	Sgt	4th Cavalry	H	11-18-1867	Altercation with Desperados. Died at Mason
McQuire	Hugh	Pvt	4th Cavalry	A	09-01-1867	Prisoner. Tried to escape and shot at San Saba Crossing
Moore *	James	Pvt	1st Infantry	A	11-01-1855	Phthisis Pulmonatic, Rheumatism
Quinn *	Patrick	Pvt	1st Infantry	F	09-08-1858	Suicide. Drowned himself in Oak Creek
Sheppard	John				6-17-1860	Killed by Indians
Taylor *	William	Pvt	8th Infantry	A	02-04-1853	Chronic Diarrhea due to dissapation
Wilson	William		4th Cavalry	A	11-00-1867	Chronic Diarrhea. Died in Austin
Wurm * ***	Daniel	Pvt		H	08-22-1867	110 mi. from Ft. Chad killed & scalped by Indians Buried: San Antonio Nat. Cem.Plot C/321

* Believed to be burried at Fort Chadbourne
** Buried at National Cemetery's

Bibliography

Old Fort Chadbourne

Bibliography

Barry, Buck - Buck Barry, Texas Ranger and Frontiersman, The Southwest Press, 1932

Bliss, Zenas R. - The Reminiscences of Major General Zenas R. Bliss 1854-1856, Texas State Historical Association, 2007

Carter, Captain R. G. - On the Border with Mackenzie, J. M. Carroll & Company, 1935

Davis, Ellis A. and Grobe, Edwin - The New Encyclopedia of Texas, Texas Development Bureau,

Dodge, Richard Irving - The Plains of the Great West, Archer House, Inc., 1877

Gray, A. B. - The A. B. Gray Report, Westernlore Press, 1963

Hume, Edgar - Ornithologist of the United States Army Medical Corps, The Johns Hopkins Press, 1942

Hunter, J. Marvin - The Trail Drivers of Texas, Cokesbury Press, 1920

Johnson, Frank – A History of Texas and Texans, American Historical Society, 1914

Johnston, William Preston, The Life of Albert Sidney Johnston, State House Press, 1997

Maddux, Vernon R. - John Hittson: Cattle King of the Texas and Colorado Frontier, University Press of Colorado, 1994

Marks, Paula Mitchell - Turn Your Eyes Toward Texas: Pioneers Sam and Mary Maverick, Texas A & M University Press, 1989

Neighbours, Kenneth Franklin - Robert Simpson Neighbors and the Texas Frontier 1836-1859, Texian Press, 1975

Ormsby, Waterman L. - The Butterfield Overland Mail, Huntington Library, 1942

Roland, Charles P. - Albert Sidney Johnston: Soldier of Three Republics, University of Texas Press, 1964

Simpson, Col. Harold B. - Cry Comanche: The 2nd U. S. Cavalry in Texas 1855-1861, Hill College Press, 1988

Smith, Thomas T. - The U. S. Army and the Texas Frontier Economy 1845-1861, Texas A&M University, 1999

Smithwick, Noah - The Evolution of a State or Recollections of Old Texas Days, University of Texas Press 1983

Stanley, David S. - Personal Memoirs Major General Davis S. Stanley, Harvard University Press, 1917

Thompson, Jerry - Civil War to the Bloody End: The Life and Times of Major Samuel P Heintzelman, Texas A&M University Press, 2006

Tompkins, G. C. - A Compendium of The Overland Mail Company on the South Route 1858-1861, G.T.Co., 1985

Wharton, Clarence R. - History of Texas, Turner Company, 1935

Williams, J. W. - Old Texas Trails, Eakin Press, 1979

War of the Rebellion: A Compilation of the Official Records of the Union and Confederate Armies, James River Publications

.

Endnotes

Old Fort Chadbourne

[1] Theodore Lincoln Chadbourne, B: 08-02-1822, Eastport, Main. Graduated West Point 1843. D: 05-09-1846 from wounds received during the battle of Resaca de la Palma.

[2] Robert Simpson Neighbors, B: 11-03-1815, Charlotte County, VA. D: 09-14-1859. Served as Indian agent in Texas and member of the Fourth Texas Legislature from 1851-1853. Shot and killed by Edward Cornett. Buried at Fort Belknap.

[3] Temporary promotion of a military officer with an increase in pay.

[4] Persifor Frazer Smith, B: 11-16-1798, Philadelphia, PA. D 05-17-1858. United States Army Officer. Commanded Department of Texas 1850-1856. Promoted to Brigadier General in 1856.

[5] U. S. 32nd Congress, 1st Session 1851:106, 117-118.

[6] Joseph Eggleston Johnston, 1807-1891. West Point Graduate. Served as Chief Topographical Engineer for the Department of Texas 1848-1853. Reached rank of General CSA, Brigadier General USA.

[7] NA, RG92, E-225, Box No. 120, Orders issued by Major General Persifor F. Smith, December 16, 1851.

[8] NA, RG391, NM-93, Entry 1270, Volume 3, Letter from Col. John Garland to Major George Deas, Assistant Adgt. General, San Antonio, Texas. July 15, 1852

[9] John Conner. B: 1802, D: 1872. Delaware scout for the military.

[10] NA, RG391, NM-93, Entry 1279, Volume Letter from Col. John Garland to Major George Deas, Assistant Adgt. General, San Antonio, Texas, July 18, 1852.

[11] Sam Cherry. Guide at Fort Chadbourne 1852, 1853. Later a guide at Fort Davis. In 1855 he was ambushed by Indians near Wild Rose Pass. His horse stumbled and fell pinning him beneath it. Cherry shot himself to avoid capture.

[12] NA, RG393, NM-93, Entry 1279, Volume 3. Letter from John Garland to Major P. Morrison, 8th Infantry.

[13] Arthur Tracy Lee. B: 06-26-1814, Northumberland, PA, D: 12-29-1879, Rochester, NY. U. S. Army Officer. Served in the 8th U. S. Infantry in the Mexican War and Civil War. Commanded Fort Chadbourne 1852. Painter and Poet. Served as Governor of the Old Soldiers Home 1867-1872 in Washington D. C. Buried Mount Hope Cemetery in Rochester, NY.

[14] Colonel Garland would be referring to 1st Lt. Edmunds B. Holloway, Quartermaster, 8th Infantry.

[15] NA, RG391, NM-93, Entry 1279, Volume 3. Letter from John Garland to Assistant Adgt. General Deas, 8th Department, San Antonio, TX, September 10. 1852.

[16] John Beardsley, B: 10-12-1816, Fairview, NY, D: 2-18-1906, Athens, NY. Graduated West Point 1841, 17th in class. Served in the Seminole, Mexican, and Civil War's. Wounded Battle of Molino del Rey. Resigned Commission in 1853. Appointed Colonel of the 9th New York Cavalry. Resigned 1863. Following his military career, he worked as a farmer.

[17] Thomas Smith, The U. S. Army & the Texas Frontier Economy 1845-1900.

[18] NA, RG391, NM-93, Entry 1270, Volume 3. Letter from John Garland to Major D.C. Buell, Assistant Adg. General, Corpus Christi, TX. March 1, 1853.

[19] NA, RG391-NM-93, Entry 1270, Volume 3. Letter from John Garland, to T. J. Wood, 2nd U. S. Dragoons, San Antonio. March 6, 1853,

[20] Washington Seawell, B: 1802 Virginia, D: 01-09-1888 San Francisco, CA. Graduated West Point 1838, 25th in Class. Served in the Mexican and Civil War. Buried Colma's Cypress Lawn Cemetery, San Francisco, CA.

[21] NA, RG391, NM-93, Entry 1279, Volume 3. Letter from John Garland to Major George Deas, August 11, 1852.

[22] William Grigsby Freeman. B: 1815, D: 11-12-1866. Made tour of inspection of the Department of Texas in 1853. Assistant Adj. General 1853-1856. Resigned 1856 due to ill health.

[23] Kenneth Franklin Neighbours, Robert Simpson Neighbors and The Texas Frontier 1836-1859.

[24] John Zirvas Leyendecker, 1827-1902. Emigrated to Texas from Germany aboard the ship Riga in 1845. Settled in Fredericksburg. He became a sutler and merchant on Oak Creek near Fort Chadbourne in 1853.

[25] Kenneth Franklin Neighbors, Robert Simpson Neighbors and the Texas Frontier 1836-1859.

[26] Discharge Paper Samuel McElroth. Garland Richards Collection, Fort Chadbourne Foundation.

[27] NA, RG 93, Letter from Captain Seth Eastman to Assistant Adjunct General, Department of Texas, June 7, 1856.

[28] Nicknamed for either a ranch hand that lived in the quarters after military years, or a close family friend whose signature appears as witness on legal documents for the Odom family.

[29] Personal Memoirs of Major-General David S. Stanley. Page 36.

[30] Letter dated June 16, 1856. M-1165, Roll #1.

[31] Jim Shaw. A Delaware Indian that served as scout and interpreter to the military on the Texas Frontier.

[32] Robert G. Hartje, Van Dorn: The Life and Times of a Confederate General.

[33] Letter dated December 17, 1865. M1165, Roll #1.

[34] NA, M 1165, Roll #1.

[35] James Morrison Hawes. B: 1824, D: 11-22-1889, Graduated West Point 1841, 29th in Class, Served Mexican and Civil War. Following his military career he was engaged in the Hardware Business. Buried Highland Cemetery, Covington, KY

[36] The A. B. Gray Report. By: Andrew Belcher Gray

[37] The Life of Albert Sidney Johnston.

[38] NA, M664, Roll 91.

[39] Richard Irving Dodge, The Plains of the Great West.

[40] History of Texas, By: Clarence Wharton

[41] John Y. Rankin, 1833-1924. Texas Ranger under Captain Giles Bogges, Company A. Served the Confederate States Army in the 25th Texas Cavalry.

[42] John Y. Rankin Diary, Henderson Rusk County Texas, 1854. Furnished by his great granddaughter Ruth Lyle.

[43] Charles Roland, Albert Sidney Johnston

[44] Will Johnston's Journal.

[45] The Reminiscences of Major General Zenas R. Bliss 1854-1876.

[46] Charles Champion Gilbert, B: 03-01-1822, Zanesville, OH, D: 01-17-1903. Graduated West Point, 1846, 21st in class. Served in the Mexican and Civil War. Served on the frontier until he retired in 1886. Buried Cave Hill Cemetery, Louisville, KY.

[47] Col. J.K.F. Mansfield's Report of the Inspection of the Department of Texas in 1856,Crimmins, Col. M. L., Southwestern Historical Quarterly, Vol. # XLII,
April 1939, Page 351.

[48] NA, M 1165, Roll #1.

[49] NA, RG112, E-12, Box No. 53.

[50] NA, RG 94, P 117, E 634, Box 24

[51] NA, M 1094, Roll #7

[52] NA, M 3316, Roll #1

[53] Old Texas Trails. By: J. W. Williams.

[54] National Archives, M 665, Roll #5

[55] Texas State Archives, RG92, Box 292.

[56] Harold B. Simpson, Cry Comanche: The 2nd U. S. Cavalry in Texas 1855-1861.

[57] NA, RG112, NM-20, Entry 208, Volume 1.

[58] NA, RG391, NM-93, Entry 1058, Volume 1

[59] Actual name was John Sheld, 1st Infantry, Company G. Reenlisted at Fort Chadbourne 4-1-1860.

[60] NA, RG 391, NM93, Entry 1058, Vol. I.

[61] Information provided by Carol Carpenter, great great great granddaughter of Dudley Johnson.

[62] John C. Robertson. B: 1824, D: 1895. Graduate of Harvard Law School. Represented Smith County during the Secession of Texas.

[63] Colonel Ben McCulloch, 1811-1862. Brother to Henry McCulloch. Authorized by Confederate President Jefferson Davis to demand the surrender of all Federal Post in Texas. Killed at the Battle of Pea Ridge, March 7, 1862.

[64] Texas and Texas, Vol. I

[65] Noah Smithwick, The Evolution of a State or Recollections of Old Texas Days.

[66] TSA, Office of Adjutants General, Box 401-843, File 843-19. Receipt for Ordnance to Captain R. B. Halley, Texas Rangers. March 28, 1861, Fort Chadbourne.

[67] War of the Rebellion, Official Records of the Union and Confederate Armies, Series II, Volume 1, Chapter 1.

[68] Davidson letters furnished by Honorable Judge John E. Sutton, San Angelo, TX.

[69] Barry 1848-1862, Box 2B44, CAH, UTA

[70] Southwestern Historical Quarterly, Vol. LIII, April 1950.

[71] Southwestern Historical Quarterly, Vol. LIII, Issue 4.

[72] National Archives, Microfilm 1165, Roll #1

[73] Appeared in Flake's Bulletin. A Galveston Newspaper from 1866-1872.

[74] Captain R. G. Carter, On the Border with Mackenzie. 1867 Post Returns.

[75] NA, M 1193, Roll 6.

[76] US 40th Congress, 2nd Session

[76] US 40th Congress, 2nd Session

[77] US 40th Congress, 3rd Session

[78] NA, M 1193, Roll 6

[79] Vernon R. Maddux, John Hittson: Cattle King on the Texas and Colorado Frontier.

[80] Robert Goldthwaite Carter. B: 10-29-1845, D: 1-4-1936. U. S. Cavalry Officer. Received the Medal of Honor for his actions during the Indian Campaign's. Late in life he became a successful author writing books based on his years in the military.

[81] The U. S. Army and the Texas Frontier Economy 1845-1900. By: Thomas Smith

[82] Leyendecker Papers, Box 2M316, CAH, UT-A

[83] Eliza Holloway letter dated April 17, 1853. Lawrence T. Jones, III Collection, Austin, TX.

[84] Eliza Holloway letter dated July 24, 1853 Garland Richards Collection, Fort Chadbourne Foundation.

[85] U. S. Army and the Texas Frontier Economy 1845-1900. By: Thomas Smith

[86] NA, RG 92, NM 81, Box 131

[87] WTHA, Vol. XV, October 1939

[88] March 7, 1853 letter from LeGrand Capers to John Leyendecker

[89] Sick and Wounded Report by Assistant Surgeon Eben Swift. December 1854.

[90] National Archives, RG 21. Eben Swift vs. Hannibal and St. Joseph Railroad Co, Case 2768. 1838-1912.

[91] Sick and Wounded Report, June 1855

[92] Edgar Erskine Hume, Ornithologist of the United States Army Medical Corps. .

[93] 1868 correspondence by Richard Kelly, brother of Michael Kelly.

[94] NA, Microfilm 1194, R 5

[95] Waterman L. Ormsby, The Butterfield Overland Mail.

[96] Barry Corbin, Actor. B: 10-16-1940 in Lamesa, Texas. Best known for his portrayal of Roscoe Brown in Lonesome Dove, and many TV series including Northern Exposure.

[97] G. C. Tompkins, Compendium of The Overland Mail Company on the South Route 1858-1861.

[98] Jerry Thompson, Civil War to the Bloody End: The Life and Times of Major General Samuel P. Heintzelman.

[99] Waterman L. Ormsby, The Butterfield Overland Mail

[100] NA, RG92, Consolidated Correspondence File, Box 292

[101] Paula Mitchell Marks, Turn Your Eyes Toward Texas: Pioneers Sam and Mary Maverick.

[102] Ellis A. Davis and Edwin H. Grobe, The New Encyclopedia of Texas. Garland G. Odom.

[103] Governor John Ireland, B: 01-01-1827, D: 03-15-1896. Served as Governor of Texas from 01-16-1883 to 01-18-1887.

[104] Texas State Archives, Letter from Thomas Lawson Odom to Governor Ireland dated February 29, 1884

[105] Texas State Archives, 401-404Court Transcripts

[106] Jimmy M. Skaggs, The Cattle-Trailing Industry Between Supply and Demand 1866-1890.

Index

A

Alabama   217
  Birmingham,   217
  Conecuh County   217
Alcohol   46-7
Alterations   91-3, 95
Ammunitions   63-4
Anderson
  George   172, 175
  William Wallace   182-3
Apaches   30
Archeological
  Excavations   190, 253, 258,
    270, 277
  Investigations   272
Arms   19, 50, 107, 112, 136-
    7, 173
Army   9, 40, 50, 83, 88, 102-
    3, 165, 181, 187, 207,
    287, 316, 322, 325
Army of Texas   54
Army Regulations   91
Arrest   14, 102-3, 223
Arrows   34, 123, 167, 171-5
Artifacts   243, 254, 270, 272,
    275
Attack, heart   246
Auctions   244, 261
Axes   19, 86

B

Babcock, William   88-9, 184
Bagby, Arthur P.   26
Baird, Spencer F.   178
Ballinger Banner   289
Baltimore   49, 51
Banking   245-6
Barb wire   221
Barber, G. C.   26

Barnes, R. S.   128-9
Barracks   63, 191, 252, 265,
    266, 267, 275
Barrett, Neil   289
Barricade   193
Barry, James Buckner   101,
    108, 127
Beardsley
  John   13-14, 17, 26, 307
  Mrs.   155
Beaumont
  Eugene B.   135-7, 143, 145,
    308-9
  Margaret   135, 145
  Natalie   135, 137
Beef   25, 74, 77, 97, 102,
    157-8
Belger, James   159
Belknap, W. W.   146
Bellamy, Asa F.   119
Bellamy Party   290
Bets   150-1
Bigham, James S.   119-20
Bills of Lading   148
Birds   178
Birth   165-6
Blake, Charles and Joy   258-
    60
Bliss, Zenus   58-9, 309, 315,
    323
Board of Survey   83
Boehm, Peter   136-7, 141,
    144, 309
Boyett
  C. W.   224, 227-8
  Neil   224, 227
Braces and turnbuckles   251,
    266
Bradfute, William B.   87, 191,
    308
Bradley, Sergeant   81

Brady, Peter Rainsford   45-6
Brands   205-6
Brandy   177
  bottles of   88-9
Bridles   85
Bronte Economic Development
     Board   257
Brooks, J. A.   127
Bruseth, Jim   267
Buell, D. C.   37, 322
Buffalo   136-7, 145, 193, 260
Buffalo Hump   10, 29, 155
Buffalo hunters   260
Bug bites   169
Building materials   8, 17, 68-
     9, 75
  Canvas   63, 66-7, 179, 267
  Flooring   20, 92-3
  Glass   67, 69
  Grout   251
  Joists   20, 22, 93
  Logs   63-7, 267
  Lumber   65
  Mortar   251-2
  Nails   69
  Penny nails   93, 95
  Pine boards   93, 95
  Rafters, pine   93, 95
  Sheathing   93, 95
  Stone   8, 17, 63, 66, 75,
     92-3, 95, 250
  Timber   8, 11, 17, 19-20,
     138, 208, 210
  Whitewash   86
Buildings   17-19, 64-5, 67, 74,
     91-3, 137-8, 152, 166,
     190, 226, 241-3, 249-50,
     267-8, 289
  Canvas roof   64-5
  Foundations   249-50, 254,
     256, 259, 261-2, 265
  Kitchen   63-4, 93, 225
  Men's barracks, enlisted   64,
     189, 250, 252, 266
  Post oak frame   75
Butrick, C. E.   269

Butterfield
  John   190
  Overland Mail   190-1, 194,
     196, 202, 325
  Overland Mail Route   190
  Stage Station   189, 202,
     252, 272-3, 275
  Stage Stop   189, 202, 252,
     272-3
  Trail   189

C

Cache   255
Cady, Robins   34-5
Calhoun, Patrick   33, 58, 307
Camp
  Abandoned Indian   128
  Colorado   78-9, 98, 116-17,
     120, 124-5
  Cooper   37-8, 40-2, 73, 77,
     117, 125, 184, 268
  Johnston   6, 8-9, 12-13, 163
  Kelly   140
  McCord   127
  McKavett   8
Campbell, Suzanne   279
Canteens   46-7, 63
Capers, LeGrand   164-5
Carpenter, Carol   103
Carpenter, J. R.   127
Carriage   163, 180
Carswell, William Amos   184
Carter, David   257, 279
Carter, Robert G.   144-5
Cathey, W. A.   128
Cattle   143, 205-6, 219, 221,
     231, 244, 282, 286
  Company   229
  Ranch   242
  Ranching   242
  Ticks   230
Cavalry
  2nd   40-1, 73, 84, 98
  4th   134-5, 139, 142, 309-
     10

Celerity 194-5
Central Hotel 224-5, 242, 287
Central Hotel - Ballinger 242
Central Hotel - Sweetwater
  224-5
Chadbourne, Theodore Lincoln
  3
Chadbourne Ranch 193, 255,
  262
Cherry, Sam 11-12, 149
Chesnut
  Dewey 254-6, 279
  Eloise 256
Chief Mulaquetop 149, 151
Children 56, 110, 116, 118-
  19, 122, 132, 135, 137,
  152, 165, 167, 169, 175,
  183, 213, 226-7
Civil War 105, 133, 136, 142,
  183, 200, 202, 218, 309-
  10, 316, 322, 325
Clark, John 142
Clifton, Elaine and Wade 275
Clothing 79
Coffee 53, 97
Coffins 56, 65
Collins, Hugh 142
Colonel Odom 218
Colts 35, 63, 257
  Army 277
  Navy 277
  Pistol 35
Comanche Springs 77
Comanche 5, 11, 29-33, 35,
  49, 53, 168-9, 172, 176,
  232, 282-4
Committee on Indian Affairs
  30
Company
  A 13, 32, 38, 51, 142
  B 38
  C 13, 51
  D 32, 58, 63, 127, 134, 141
  E 42, 212
  F 32, 34, 38, 51, 58, 63-4,
    81, 83, 170

G 13, 38, 51, 96, 98, 110,
  112, 134, 177
H 42, 127, 134, 141
I 13, 41
K 13, 51
Concho Valley Archeological
  Society 253, 258
Concho Valley RC&D 256
Cone, Aurelius 88
Confederate
  Camp 129
  States Army 108, 112, 119,
    185, 218, 323
  Troops 127
Confederates 131
Conkling, Roscoe P. 202
Conner, John 8, 11, 321
Contract, wagon freight 159
Convention 106
Cook, W. P. 82
Cooper, Samuel 40
Corbin, Barry 196, 257
Corn 25, 65, 118, 134, 157,
  164
Corral 189, 196, 198, 273
Correspondence 36-7, 86, 89,
  115, 133, 146, 154, 156,
  164, 167, 193, 212, 233,
  325
County
  Bexar 205, 207, 218
  Brown 127
  Callahan 227
  Coke 13, 144-5, 219, 260
  Comanche 128
  Coryell 128
  Erath 128
  Garza 229-30
  Henderson Rusk 323
  Jacks 140
  Johnson 128
  Nolan 219, 224, 228
  Runnels 219, 223, 232-3,
    241, 288
  Taylor 219, 227
  Throckmorton 30, 140

Tom Green   6, 126, 140,
    145, 219
Young   8, 30
County Commissioner   220
Court Martial   101, 104
Cowan, D. C.   108
Cowboys   193, 260, 275
Cowboys and Indians   213
Creek
  Asylum   124
  Bluff   77-8
  Brady's   78, 160
  Oak Creek   13, 22, 48, 54,
    76, 78, 172, 206-7, 219,
    322
  Pecan   160
  Valley   78, 219
Crigler
  Judge Ruben and Eleanor
    241
  Sallie M.   241
Culver, William H.   128-9
Cunningham, James   128
Cureton, Jack   127
Currie, Nettie   243

D

Dallas Daily Herald   287-8
Dallas Morning News   289
Dallas Weekly Herald   285
Daniel, September   279
Davidson
  Mary   115-16, 118, 120
  Sidney Green   115-16, 121-
    4
Davidson's Company   117,
    119
Davis
  Samuel Boyer   212
  W. T.   254, 279
Deas, George   8
Delaware Indians   8, 323
Department of Interior   82
Department of Texas   19, 26,
    29, 32-4, 37, 42, 48, 51,

73-4, 80-1, 106, 109,
    180, 186, 210, 321-3
Dereson, Jesse A.   119, 185
Desertions   63
Devine, Thomas J.   107
Disease   4, 162, 169, 187,
    231-2
  Cholera   169
  Colds, common   169
  Constipation   169
  Contusions   169
  Diarrhea   169
  Digestive disorders   169
  Drunkenness   169
  Fractures   169
  Gangrene   177
  Rheumatism   169
  Scurvy   169
  Smallpox   169
  Tuberculosis   169
District of Texas   133, 187
Dodge, Richard Irving   26,
    149, 315
Dodge Jones Foundation   252,
    256
Donahue, Patrick   100
Double Officer's Quarters   xiii,
    166, 252, 270-1
Dove Creek   126-7, 129-33
Dowser   254
Dragoons   32, 45, 51, 58,
    171, 177, 179, 191, 282-
    3, 322
  2nd   32, 51, 58, 171, 310
Drummer, John   297, 299
Dumreicher, Conrad C.   186-8

E

East Barracks   265-7, 275
Eastman, Seth   34-6, 58, 61-
    2, 181, 307
Eighth Military Department   5
Eighth Texas Cavalry Battalion
    125
Erwin, Ralph   246

Extra duty men   81

F

Farmers and Merchants Bank
   242
Farming   164-5
Fashion   111
Federal
   Forces   109
   Post in Texas   324
   Troops   42, 106-7, 117,
      128, 134, 144, 293
Fence   208-9, 220-3, 226,
   230, 232, 288
   Cutters   220, 222, 229
   Cutting   220, 223, 232
Fifth Military District   140
Fink, T.   27
First Frontier District   127
First National Bank of Ballinger
   246
First Texas Cavalry   125
Fish Creek   77-8
   Fence Cutters Gang   223
   Gang   224
Flannigan, R. L.   279
Flour   53, 150, 285
Follett, F. M.   27
Forage   6, 74, 76
Fort
   Belknap   5, 30-1, 44, 56,
      80, 82, 87-8, 125, 127,
      184, 282, 285, 321
   Brown   81-2, 139
   Chadbourne   iii-v, vii-ix, 31-
      9, 54-9, 85-91, 107-13,
      139-49, 156-61, 163-8,
      177-83, 185-6, 190-6,
      199-202, 252-8, 260-2,
      281-7
   Phantom Hill   5, 12, 56, 77
   Clark   5, 80, 286
   Concho   13, 140, 144
   Cooper   80
   Croghan   5

Davis   80, 321
Gates   5
Graham   5
Griffin   140
Harker   162
Hudson   80
Inge   48, 80
Lancaster   80
Martin Scott   5, 18-19, 27,
   162
Mason   5, 34, 38, 45, 61,
   78, 80, 82, 125, 134, 159,
   184, 188
McIntosh   81-2
McKavett   5, 9, 27, 34, 48,
   56, 58, 70, 78, 80, 82,
   159, 286
Phantom Hill   5, 9, 12-13,
   56, 77, 146
Richardson   140, 144
Terrett   5
Verde   80
Worth   5, 279
Yuma   82
Fort Chadbourne
   Artillery   254
   Cavalry   254
   Cemetery   234
   Commanders   80, 143, 307
   Days   260
   Foundation   v, viii, 139, 256,
      259-61, 279, 322, 325
   Guard House and Prison   65
   Roster of Federal Troops
      293-301
   Roster of Soldiers   293
   Roster of Texas Regimental
      Troops   303
   Visitor's Center   275-6
Fossett, Henry   127-30, 132
Foundation Certificate of
   Incorporation   252
Fountain House   36, 268-9
Fourth Texas Legislature   4,
   321
Franklin, Nathal J.   119

Frazer, Gay   279
Freeman, Joe   22-5, 251
Freeman, W. G.   22-5
Frontier   4, 9, 35, 41-3, 49,
    51, 81, 86, 90, 96, 106,
    109, 126, 132, 134-5, 152
  Forts   24, 56, 90, 178, 218
Frost, Thomas   108, 117, 120-
    1, 123-4
Fuel   6, 73-4, 76, 208

G

Gallatin, Samuel   119
Gamblers   198-200
  French   197-8
Gambling
  Money   96-7
Garden   59, 102, 179
Garland, John   6, 8, 11-12,
    14, 18, 24, 26, 146, 166,
    239, 241, 245, 249-51,
    270, 321-2
Garrisons   4, 9, 18, 81, 150,
    155, 174, 282-3
Garza, Jesus   206
Gehring, William   83
General Order
  No 3   165
Geneva College   181
Giddens, J. R.   127
Gilbert, Charles   307
Gill, Kelly   279
Gillespie, J. T.   223
Gillintine, N. M.   127, 129
Glenn, Mary Frances   279
Gooch, I. C.   77
Good, F. H.   100
Goodnight, Charles   143, 230
Governor Ireland   222, 326
Governor of Texas   105, 326
Graffiti   269
Graham, G.   128
Granary   66
Grant, Ulysses S.   139
Grass   77-8, 138, 160, 195

Gray, A. B.   45-6, 201, 284
Green, Billy   170
Green Lake   110
Griffin, Charles   133
Guard house   20-1, 67
Guides   11
Guion, Neil   290
Gunfight 200
Guns 277, 309-310
  Antique Displays   260
  Black Powder   260

H

Hailstones   48
Haines, John   34-5
Halley, Robert Bonner   108-
    10, 116, 308
Hamilton, Wiley   119
Hamner, H. A.   108
Haneman, Albert   265
Hanlon, Thomas   96, 101
Hardy's Station   285
Harness Store   66
Harper's Ferry Muskets   23
Harrison, Thomas   108
Harry Holt Award   245
Hartsuff, George   133, 188
Hatch, John   133
Hatchets   86
Hawes, James   45-6, 307
Hay   25, 65-6, 74, 77, 86,
    134, 157-8, 210
Hedges, Joseph   310
Heintzelman, Samuel Peter
    200
Hemphill, William C.   137
Historic Preservation Act   262
Holloway
  Edmunds B.   12, 25, 154,
    157, 321
  Eliza   154, 156-7, 325
Holman, J. H.   83
Hood, John Bell   14
Horace   113
Horse   83, 130

Mare   151
  Race   147, 149-52
Hospital   18, 20-3, 64-5, 67,
    74, 92, 171-2, 252
Houston, Sam   105
Howard, Agent   32
Howard, Mr.   210
Howard, Richard A.   148
Howard, T.   159
Howitzers, twelve pound   109
Hoyt, Alexander   90
Humble Oil Company   254
Hume, Edgar Erskine   178
Hurricane   162
Huston, Daniel   100

I

Illinois Volunteers   186
Indian
  Accounts   149
  Camp   130
  Campaign   325
  Department of Texas   35
  Depredations   34, 43, 86,
    232
  Encampments   132
  Headdresses   155
  Hostile raids   4
  Pony   150
  Raids   48
  Reservations, establishing   4
  Territory   30, 43, 144, 163
  Woman   39
Indian Affairs   30
  Superintendent of   9
Indian Agent in Texas   283
Indians   4-5, 9-11, 29-31, 34-
    40, 43-4, 59, 61, 81, 101,
    121, 123-4, 126-7, 129-
    32, 141-3, 148-52, 154-7
  Delaware   8
  Reservation   43
Infantry   6, 9, 20, 25, 34, 41,
    43, 58, 62, 79-81, 83, 98-

101, 109-12, 140, 297-8,
    321
  1st   34, 41, 58, 74-5, 88,
    98, 109, 111
  8th   6, 9-10, 13-14, 20, 51,
    157, 163, 309
Ireland, Gov. John   220, 222
Iron bedsteads   63-4, 88

J

JA Ranch   230
James Gross Survey   213
Jay Rollins Library   243
Jessup, Thomas   159, 210
Johnson
  Dudley   101-3
  Roberta Cole   257-8
Johnston
  Albert Sidney   34, 40, 56-7,
    316, 323
  Eliza   56
  Joseph Eggleston   6
  Will   57

K

Kansas   219, 229
Kelly, Michael J.   140, 186
Kenney, James   i, 257
Keogh, Miles   14
Ketumpsee   10
Ketumse   31
Kickapoo   13
  Creek   78
  Springs   8-9
Kickapoo Indians   131
King, John H.   41, 79-80, 307-
    8
Kiowa   5, 31, 53-4
Konczak Foundation   256
Kuykendall
  G. R.   119
  Mary   116

335

L

Land   30-1, 76, 148, 205-10, 213, 218-21, 230-1, 233, 250
Lane, E. D.   58, 148
Langworthy, Elisha P.   62, 64, 67, 69-70, 180-1
Laths   21
Laundresses   63, 89-92, 110
Lawhon, Mary (Sug)   i
Lawson, T.   167
Lawson, Thomas   178
Leach, James B.   82-3
Leath, Thomas   119
Lee
  Arthur Tracy   11-12, 26, 307
  Pat   279
  Robert E.   14, 37, 39-40, 268
Leigh, A. K.   109, 170
Leyendecker, John   148, 153-4, 164
Leyendecker Papers   148
Lindsey, E. A.   219
Livestock   230, 232
Longstreet, James   13, 27
The Lost Fort   257
Loving, Oliver   143-4
Luckett
  Henry H.   229
  P. N.   107
Ludlow, Henry   119

M

Mackenzie, Ranald   132, 144-5, 315, 324
Mackey, Columbus   119
Magnetometer survey   267
Mansfield, J. K. F.   x, xii, 61-4, 66-7
Marcy, Randolph   30-1, 211, 282

Maroney, John   141
Marriage   233, 241-2
Marshal, James C.   119
Martin
  Gilbert   170
  Louis   77
Massacre   132, 283
Mather, Mr.   194
Mathews, Kennie   279
Matlock, Ruben   171-2, 175
Maverick
  George M.   212
  Lewis   212
  Mary   211
  Samuel Augustus   76, 106, 205-12, 219, 287
Maynard's primer muskets   24
McCaleb, Mary Hunt   233
McCord, James E.   219
McCulloch
  Ben   107-8, 125
  Henry   108-9, 116, 120, 125, 212
McFalls, Thaddeus B.   139
McIntosh, James   26
McKay's Ranch   78
McMurry College   243
McNair, Duncan   119
Medal of Honor   257, 275, 309-10, 325
Mercedes, Jose   206
Merchant, C. G.   26
Mercy Hospital   188
Mexican War   3, 162, 184
Michell, Tobias   73-4, 183, 185
Michigan, Tecumseh   269
Military records   103-4, 176, 189, 193
Miller, Andrew G.   61, 66, 68, 79, 307
Millican, Jo   258
Milstead, Lucinda S.   217
Mirror, John   177
Missouri   173, 190-1, 197
Missouri, St. Joseph   173

Mohawk   111
Morphine   177
Morris
  Gouverneur   101, 109-10,
    308
  R. C.   119
Morrison, Pitcairn   307
Mountain
  Margaret   144
  Round   78
Mountain howitzers   109
Mulaquetop   149
Mules   25, 47, 56, 65, 83,
    194-5, 211, 232, 272
Murray, William   87
Musicians   62
Myers, A. C.   67, 207

N

National Archives   324-5
Nayler, Columbus   119
Negro slave   57
Neighbors, Robert Simpson   4,
    29-33, 43-4, 258, 316,
    321-2
New Orleans   133
New York   113
New York Herald   190
Newton, W. J.   31, 33
Nichols, Mr.   194
NRA Foundation   257

O

O D Ranch   241
Oak Creek Store   148
Oakwood Cemetery   234
Oaths   112-13
Odom
  Ancelia   217
  Cyrus Wallace   217
  Edna M.   241-2
  Garland   166, 217, 219,
    229-30, 236, 241, 251,
    268, 270, 289

George Washington   217
John M.   217
John Patrick   217
Lou Nettie   241
Lucinda   213, 233, 241, 270
Lula M.   217
Mary Hunt McCaleb   234
Nelly   217
Sallie   166, 241
Sallie Crigler   166, 236, 241
Sarah Frances   217
Sedonia K.   217
Stephen A.   217
Thomas Lawson   213, 217,
    220-226, 229-230, 232
Thomas Lawson Jr.   217
William Edgar   217
Odom Luckett Land and Cattle
    Company   229
O'Donnell Foundation   257
Officers Quarters   20-1, 36,
    67-8, 75, 93, 138, 252-
    253, 268-9, 271, 289
O'Hara, Theodore   38-40
Oil   vii-viii
Oklahoma   44
Ormsby, Waterman L.   190-1,
    193-5, 316, 325
Ornithologist   178, 182, 315,
    325
Oxen   168, 285

P

Pace, Edward   119
Panthers   170
Parade grounds   22, 136, 145,
    181, 188, 191, 193
Parker, Cynthia Ann   144
Pate
  Ann   iv, ix, 279
  Randall   i
Patent   206, 208
Pearce, F. M.   246
Pease, Governor   32
Percussion Lock   23

Perini, Tom   279
Phillips, E. D.   85, 91-2
Piazzas   11, 20-1
Pickett, George E.   26
Pierson, Bill   267
Pin, picket   135-6
Pitcher,Thomas G.   26
Poehls, Ronnie   279
Post
  Chaplain   73
  First Sutler   148
  Sutler   147, 164
Preservation Texas Award
  251, 266
Prison   65, 227-8
Prisoners   11, 65, 112, 310
Punch, milk   46

Q

Quinine   177

R

Ragsdal, Bill   55
Railroad   173-5, 232
Rain gauge   89, 168-9
Ranch   viii, 219, 231, 241-3,
  245-6, 254
Ranchers   222, 229-32, 244,
  251
Ranching   229, 241, 245, 275
Ranching Headquarters   241
Rancier, Edward   119
Rangers   43, 101, 109, 118,
  283, 287
Rankin, John Y.   55
Rations   17
Red Fork   211
Red Horse   269
Reeves, Beverly   279
Register of Historic Places   262
Revolvers   36, 198-9
Reynolds, Samuel H.   83, 308
Richards
  Brian   245-6

Conda   275
Edmund "Bud"   245
Garland   i, v, vii-viii, 239,
  245-6, 249-50, 262, 266,
  279
Lana   i, iii, 246, 249-50,
  262, 279
Nell Papasan   238, 245
Sallie   245
Riemenschneider, Larry   253
Rifle Musket   91
Ringgold Barracks   51, 81-2
River
  Brazos   12, 43, 87, 140
  Colorado   8, 11, 34, 38, 45,
    76, 78-9, 82, 121, 123,
    128, 160, 206-7, 211
  Concho   6, 13, 45, 47, 78-9,
    124-5, 134, 139, 160, 256
  Mississippi   113
  North Concho   6, 8, 11, 128,
    140, 142
  Red   31, 40, 43, 108, 120
  Rio Concho   134
  Rio Grande   51, 82
  San Saba   6, 78, 159
Robertson, John C.   106
Rodents   251
Root Cellar   252, 274
Round Up For Rehab   244
Rusty Spur Productions   257

S

Saddles   85, 231, 243, 272
San Antonio Depot   33
San Antonio Express   286-7
San Francisco   186, 190, 196,
  202, 322
Sanaco   10, 29, 31, 35, 38-9,
  53-4, 149, 155, 169
Sandstone   75, 189
Satanta   54
Schooners   111
Schuchard, Charles   201
Scott, Jeremiah D.   119

Scott, Robert 119
Scouting trips 128
Seawell, Washington 25, 206, 307
Secession of Texas 324
Selden, J. 27
Sharps 51, 257
Sharps rifle 277
Shaw, Jim 38
Sheld, John 98, 101-2, 324
Shelton, Samuel 119
Sherry 88
Shingles 10, 18-19, 22, 64-8, 93, 95, 199, 218
Ships 111
Sibley, Caleb 110-12
Single Officers Quarters 252
SMARTS 253
Smith
  Charles 89
  Charles Henry 184
  E. K. 98
  Larkin 26
  Malacthon 26
  Persifor 5-6, 32, 37, 48, 210
  Shelly 243-4
  Thomas 322, 325
Smithsonian Institute 201
Smithwick, Noah 108
Smoking 197, 224
Snelling, J. G. S. 26
Sons of Malta 59
South Carolina 182, 184
Southern Comanches 32-3
Southwestern Historical Quarterly 323-4
Special Order
  No. 13 134
  No. 27 140
Spinners 260
Spur Ranch 229-31
St. Joseph 173-4
St. Joseph Railroad Company 173
St. Louis 95, 190, 197, 202

St. Louis Republican 117
Stage
  Drivers 194, 199-200
  Stop 189-90, 197, 200, 272-3
Stagecoach 191-2, 194-5, 197, 272-3
Stanley, David S. 171-3, 175, 310, 316
Star of the West 111
State Militia 131
State of Texas iii, 106, 126, 220, 252, 262, 273
State Troops 128-9, 131
Station keeper 194, 196, 200, 272
Steuart, George 49-51
Stone masons 17
Stove 224-6
Sugar 53, 150, 157
Summerfield G. Roberts Foundation 256
Summerlee Foundation 256
Surrender 35-6, 106-10, 324
Survey of Land 208-9
Sutler 58
Sweet, Jas R. 154
Swift
  Eben 26, 48, 55-6, 149, 161, 165-9, 172, 174-5, 180-3, 193, 307, 325
  Ezra and Lucy 162
  Sarah Edwards Capers 162-5, 174, 180

T

Teamsters 19, 24, 65, 81, 101, 159, 250
Temperature 46-7
Tents 22, 37, 80, 164, 167, 179, 184
Texas 5, 8, 37-8, 40-3, 75-6, 106-8, 132-4, 139-41, 181-4, 206-8, 217-18,

220-1, 232-4, 260-2, 315-
17, 321-5
Abilene 5
Albany 140
Austin 106, 116
Ballinger 241-3, 275, 289
Bastrop 75-6
Big Spring 123-4
Bronte 5
Brownsville 108, 139
Brownwood 116-17
Burnett 5
El Paso 51
Fever 230
Fredericksburg 5, 17, 45,
66, 76, 148, 153, 159,
162-4, 322
Galveston 113
Huntsville 54
Indianola 158
Jacksboro 140
Menard 5
San Angelo 140
San Antonio 5, 8, 14, 25,
45, 50-1, 62, 65-6, 69,
106-7, 158-9, 180-1, 212,
218-19, 286-7, 321-2
Sonora 5
Sweetwater 224
Tomball 255
Texas and Pacific Railroad
Company 146
Texas Convict Records Ledger
227
Texas Development Bureau
315
Texas Historical Commission
253, 256, 267
Texas Legislature 220, 222
Texas Ordinance of Secession
5, 106
Texas Rangers 54, 56, 101,
223, 227-8, 323-4
Texas State Archives 324,
326
Texas State Gazette 282

Texas Troops
Army 109
Cavalry 218, 323
Militia 127
Mounted Rangers 109
Mounted Riflemen 110, 212
Mounted Rifles 116-17,
119, 185, 301, 303
Mounted Volunteers 32, 42,
87
Regimental Forces 108
Regimental Troops 303,
308
Troops 107
Volunteers 33
Texas Western Railroad 284
Texas Western Railroad
Company 45
Thomas, C. W. vii, 35-6, 62,
65-7, 69, 83, 85, 213,
217, 230, 233, 241, 297-
9, 301, 303, 308
Thomas, George 41
Tiaquash, Chief 50
Ticks 231
Toole, Mrs. 89
Totton, S. S. 128-30, 132
Trade 153-6
Traders 152-3
Trail Drivers of Texas 315
Tucker, Dr. 196-200
Twiggs, David 42-3, 80-1,
107
Twohig, Mr. 210

U

United States
Army Medical Corps 178,
182, 325
Government 29-30, 106,
206
Post Office 274
United States Army 80, 112,
162, 178, 181, 183-4
Urbana 111

V

Van Dorn, Earl 14, 37, 39-40, 84, 111-112, 184, 323
Vandever, L. 158
Venereal disease
  Gonorrhea 169
  Syphilis 169
Vinon, D. H. 74
Visitor's Center 267, 275-6
Volunteers 33, 54, 116, 186, 253, 256, 261-2

W

Wagon train 82
Wagons 51, 79
Waite, Carlos A. 107, 110
Wallace, George 89-91, 95-6, 308
Wareham, Massachusetts 161
Warren
  Benjamin G. 223-8, 287-8
  Eppie Hubbert 227
  George 119
Warren Wagon Train Massacre 144
Washington, T. A. 62, 73-4, 79, 308
West Texas 46
West Texas Rehabilitation Center 243, 245
Wheeler, Mr. 194, 196
Whiskey, bottles of 88-9
Wild Indians 49, 149
Winchester Quarantine 230
Winchester rifles 230
Windmill
  Eclipse 275
Wine, bottles of 88-9
Wint, Theodore J. 137, 188
Winter 49, 53, 56, 73, 160, 279

Witcher 254
Witching stick 254
Withers, John 80, 98
Wolff, Anton Frederick 148, 153
Wood, Henry Clay 310
Wood, L. B. 26, 307
Wood, W. J. 227, 289
Work
  Undercover 222-3
  Volunteer 254
Wounded Report 167, 325
Wounds 171-2, 224, 321
  Arrow 144, 171, 173
Wurm, Daniel 141
Wylie
  Conda 237, 242-246
  Edna 243
  Maurine 245

Y

Yager rifles 35
Yellow Wolf 155

Z

Zappe Saloon 275